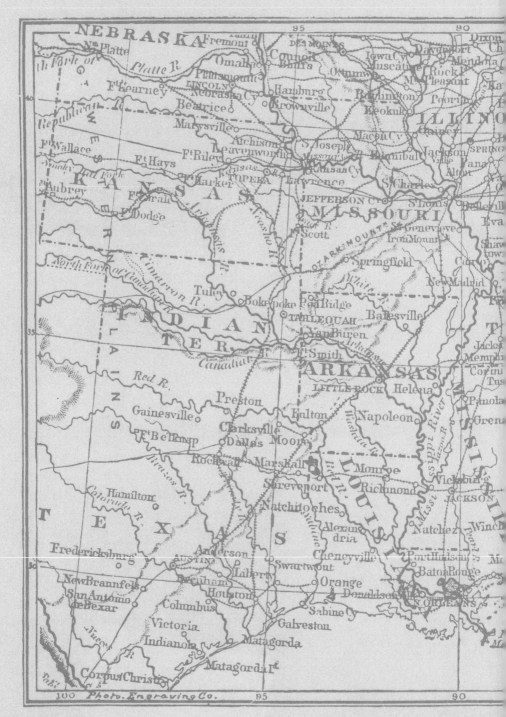

GENERAL MAP OF

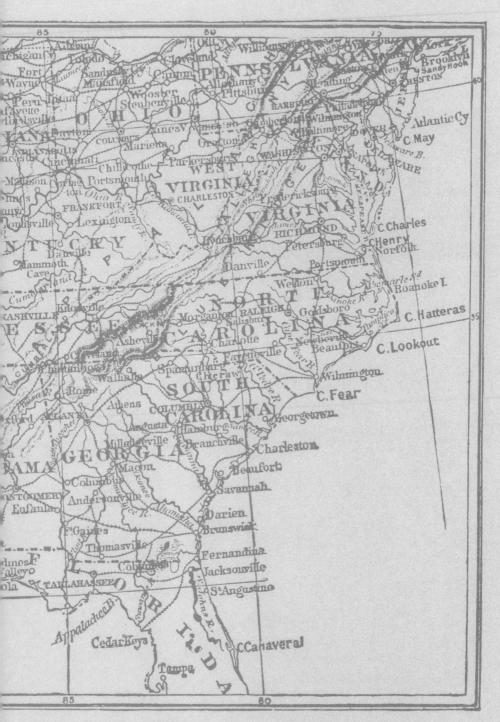

OUTHERN STATES.

Tara Revisited

∽

WOMEN,
WAR,
& THE
PLANTATION
LEGEND

Tara Revisited

WOMEN,
WAR,
& THE
PLANTATION
LEGEND

Catherine Clinton

Abbeville Press   Publishers
New York   London   Paris

Editor: Constance Herndon
Designer: Celia Fuller
Production Editor: Owen Dugan
Picture Editor: Laura Straus
Production Manager: Lou Bilka

First paperback edition
2 4 6 8 10 9 7 5 3

Library of Congress Cataloging-in-Publication Data
Clinton, Catherine, 1952–
Tara revisited : women, war & the plantation legend /
Catherine Clinton — 1st ed.
p.   cm.
Includes bibliographical references and index.
ISBN 0-7892-0159-3
1. United States—History—Civil War, 1861–1865—Women.   2. Women—
Confederate States of America.   3. Plantation life—Southern States—
History—19th century.   4. Women—Southern States—History—
19th century.   I. Title.
E628.C58   1995
973.7'15042—dc20   94-39218

Contents

Dedicated to
Aida and David Donald
with
abiding affection
for our
afternoons in Lincoln
past and future

ℒ

Acknowledgments

⁓

P reparing to thank the enormous number of people who helped to make *Tara Revisited* possible is a daunting task. It is one of the great rewards of doing research for a book like this that so many people open their archives and photo collections, their files and memory banks to share so generously. The kindness of those whose names follow made my undertaking over the past decade much easier, more pleasant, as well as more challenging. I'm afraid of committing sins of omission, but at the same time, I want to acknowledge so many who contributed, especially the kindnesses extended by the staffs of the United Daughters of the Confederacy in Richmond, the Southern Historical Collection at the University of North Carolina (Chapel Hill), the South Carolina Historical Society in Charleston, the United States Military History Institute in Carlisle, Pennsylvania, the Natchez Trace Collection at the University of Texas, Austin, the Caroliniana Library at the University of South Carolina, Columbia, the Mississippi State Archives, Jackson, the Virginia Historical Society, Richmond, the Virginia State Library, Richmond, the Historic New Orleans Collection, the Woodruff Library at Emory University, the National Archives, and most especially, the Library of Congress, with special thanks to Mary Ison. Invitations from both Clemson University and the College of Charleston over the years have been welcome excuses to visit valued colleagues, drop into archives, and enjoy Carolina hospitality which lives up to its legendary reputation. I owe an enormous debt as well to Randolph-Macon Woman's College in Lynchburg, Virginia, which hosted me on research forays; I encourage others to visit their splendid Collection of the Writings of Virginia Women. Frances White Webb, who called my attention to this treasure trove, Ruth Anne Edwards, and Nancy Gray were all instrumental in making my visits such enjoyable research excursions.

Special mention must be made of those who were so generous with assistance as I was seeking illustrations and other material for my book over the years: Lawrence Strichman, Diane B. Jacobs, Arthur Barrett, John A. Martin, Jr., Dick Schrader, Harriet McDougal, David Moltke-Hansen, Charles Reagan Wilson, Anne Marie Price, Mark Wetherington, Devon Goddard, Guy Swanson, Diana Arecco, Jim Heisler, Jamila Jefferson, Jo Anne Kendall, Randy Sparks, Kathy Haldane, Leah Arroyo, Joan Cashin, Ken Greenberg, Carol Bleser, Jean Baker, Susanna Delfino, Lee Ann Whites, Bennett Singer, Nicoletta Karam, Michael Melcher, Pilar Olivo, Lisa Cardyn, and, most especially, Corrine Hudgins of the Museum of the Confederacy.

Many at Abbeville Press deserve appreciation and praise. First and foremost, I salute Mark Magowan, whose vision shaped the book from the outset and whose championing of the project has been invaluable. I remain much indebted to the editorial skills of Constance Herndon, whose talents measurably improved the manuscript. Celia Fuller's indelible influence is evident from cover to cover; she was a terrific designer for this project, particularly attuned to the book's (and my own) demanding requirements. I also want to thank Walton Rawls, Laura Straus, and Owen Dugan, with special gratitude for Mary Christian's numerous and critical contributions at the final stages of the project.

The many hosts who have fed and sheltered me while completing my work are legendary: Jane Gottlieb and David Obst, Christine Heyrman and Tom Carter, Barbara and Paul Uhlmann, Jr., Clara and Richard Crockatt, Cora and Winthrop Jordan, Paul and Bobbie

Simms, Jeffrey and Deborah Tatro, Constance Schultz, Fran and Emory Thomas, Marie Tyler-McGraw, Patricia Montgomery, Gene Roe, Pilar Viladas, and most especially, Nicholas G. Harris. Finally, I can never hope to repay a couple who has been rolling out the red carpet for me in D.C. for over two decades: Craig and Fran D'Ooge, along with their daughters, Charlotte and Justine.

My mother, Claudene Clinton, has been a generous fan over the last six books, and I hope she will continue her boundless enthusiasm for the next half-dozen as well. My father-in-law, Edwin Colbert, cheerfully parted with his facsimile copies of *Harper's Weekly* for the Civil War years, a loan that was much appreciated. My husband, Daniel Colbert, and our two sons, Drew and Ned, were not so cheerful to part with me, as was frequently required for the sake of this project. During 1992 alone, I made twelve research trips, on top of my weekly commute to Cambridge for teaching, making theirs an extraordinary sacrifice, for which I remain, as always, in their debt.

CATHERINE CLINTON
Riverside, Connecticut

Foreword

Of the various communities of agents that created nineteenth-century American life, it is the inner lives of women, along with those of people of color, which remain largely *terra incognita* even to late twentieth-century readers. And of the various communities of nineteenth-century women, none is more complex or enigmatic than that of women in the South. How did women construct their social and psychological identities within the confines of fixed and repressive stereotypes and occupational roles that sought to delimit even the possibilities of that to which a woman could aspire? And how did southern women and men—and white women and black women in the South—construct each other, mutually constitute each other, in a dialectical dance of sameness and difference that racialized American sexual relations, while at the same time sexualizing American race relations?

These questions, and others, are explored in magnificent detail in Catherine Clinton's *Tara Revisited: Women, War, & the Plantation Legend.* Unfolding her tale against the myth of a phantasmagoric "Old South," Clinton explores the nature and effects of war—here, the Civil War—on the fabric of gender relations, both between the sexes and within the white and black female communities. Not only is this book a germinal contribution to women's history, it is also a subtle and often brilliant meditation upon the shaping structures of war itself. In her sensitive excavations of life along the southern plantations' gendered color-line, *Tara Revisited* is a model of a historical text well-conceived and splendidly executed.

HENRY LOUIS GATES, JR.

Of Legends and Plantations

Of Legends
and Plantations

T he most famous plantation in the American South never existed. The mythical Tara was a series of iconographic images conjured from fact and fiction, a celluloid dream for some and a nightmarish caricature for others. Mementos and misremembering, pride and prejudices, were mixed into the historical batter and served up as legend to hungry fans. Every year hundreds, perhaps thousands of visitors flock to Georgia and inquire, "Where's Tara?"

This book is not an attempt to *find* Tara but to relocate the legend in a complex interweaving of myth and memories, particularly in relation to the lives of Southern women. The creation and evolution of the legendary Old South will be as important to this exploration as the harrowing and heartening tales of women who lived through the rise and fall of the Confederacy. Despite the myth that will serve as backdrop, the book will focus primarily on the actual impact of the war upon real women during the battle for Confederate independence, a battle that was simultaneously the struggle for black emancipation.

Despite the considerable mists of sentiment that have clouded this chapter of the Southern past, stories of women's courage and female heroics are riveting and relatively unheralded. Many tales need no embellishment to wring empathy from a reader. Yet the creative bending of the truth to suit poetic license in Civil War literature strikes a

---

powerful chord for many Americans. The images of Scarlett, Mammy, and other women of plantation lore still hold us in their thrall. But before analyzing the realm of myth and folklore, I will explore the lives of those real women whose experiences illuminate our appreciation of the Civil War past.

In order to convey something of the realities of plantation life, *Tara Revisited* will chronicle challenges confronted by Southern plantation women with the outbreak of the Civil War, sketching dilemmas faced by all plantation women, black and white, and exploring their struggles with one another. The secession of the Southern states and the formation of the Confederacy was one of the most dramatic chapters in the American past, one that has inspired thousands of books. But despite the fascination this period holds for readers and scholars, aspects of it remain trivialized. Indeed, the topic of women's responses to and roles in the Civil War—so long a popular theme in fiction and film—has only just begun to blossom in scholarly literature.

Despite this academic neglect, publishers long ago discovered the magnetism of Civil War memoirs. Although Abraham Lincoln—a symbol of triumph and tragedy for the Union—reigns supreme within the field, the Southern experience has been well represented in historical and popular writing. In particular, Confederate women have provided us with a steady stream of important historical characters—from the fascinating Jones family women introduced in the prize-winning *Children of Pride* (1972) to the equally beguiling Mary Boykin Chesnut, whose story earned C. Vann Woodward a Pulitzer Prize in 1982 with *Mary Chesnut's Civil War.*

The lives of black Southern women, on the other hand, remain obscured and uncelebrated. Too little evidence remains on slave and freedwomen. And so, to a great extent, we must extrapolate the experiences of African-American women from African Americans in general. The National Archives have provided a treasure trove illuminating black experience during this dynamic era. The heroism of the black soldier during the Civil War, so long a forgotten chapter of our past, has enjoyed a new popularity. This powerful image was highlighted when Denzel Washington won an Academy Award for his performance in *Glory* (1989), a film featuring the experience of black soldiers in the Union army. The dramatic impact of the war on Southern slaves and the struggle for freedom waged by blacks within the Confederacy continues as a vital legacy of the Civil War.

The intensity of this experience is revealed in the voices of thou-

sands of former slaves—women and men—interviewed during the Depression for a Works Progress Administration (WPA) project sometimes referred to as "the slave narratives." Also, the millions of documents collected and recorded by the Bureau of Refugees, Freedmen and Abandoned Lands, familiarly known as the Freedman's Bureau, have also been surveyed, processed, and edited for publication in an ambitious multi-volume work entitled *Freedom: A Documentary History of Emancipation* (1861–1867). This sampling affords us precious insight into the obstacles and opportunities confronted by newly-emancipated blacks, both women and men.

Still, the pages of history remain overcrowded with material drawn too heavily from white interpretations of black experience and from Confederate perspectives on events. As we well know, the meanings of war are as varied as those individuals who experience it. Our rich storehouse of documentary sources allow us to explore multiple voices and alternative views of this watershed event. These stories will perhaps never be woven into one smooth narrative that can satisfy both North and South, black and white, male and female, or any of the other divides that predated the war and survived the struggle. By allowing diverse and even clashing perspectives to emerge, however, we can create an historical mosaic that pieces together the meanings of the conflict for us several generations later. And we can come to hear the historical voices of black women, so long muffled by the din of alternate interpretations, incorporating their roles into this emblematic era.

The Civil War still exerts gravity—both a pull and a weight on the late twentieth century. Even in 1988, more than fifty thousand gathered at Gettysburg for a re-enactment of the battle on its one hundred and twenty-fifth anniversary. This crowd was even more diverse than those

---

ABOVE: PRIDE OF MOTHERHOOD IS REFLECTED IN THIS POST–CIVIL WAR PORTRAIT OF AN UNIDENTIFIED BLACK MOTHER WITH HER INFANT.

who fought near Little Round Top in 1863. Costumed participants mingled with the crowd of observers who had flocked to watch the event, in an atmosphere reminiscent of that surrounding the first Battle of Bull Run, when festive picnickers and ladies in carriages drove out from Washington to see the show in July 1861. The modern re-enactment of Gettysburg brought old and young, predominantly men, but many women, and almost all whites. (Of the less than fifty blacks at the site, most were members of the media.) This group reflected the spirit of those who wanted not just to commemorate history, but to relive it.

As William Faulkner wrote about Gettysburg in *Intruder in the Dust* (1948): "For every Southern boy fourteen years old not once but whenever he wants it, there is the instant when it's still not yet two o'clock on that July afternoon in 1863, the brigades are in position behind the rail fence, the guns are laid and ready in the woods . . . and Pickett himself . . . with his hat in one hand . . . and his sword in the other looking up the hill waiting for Longstreet to give the word and

LABORERS RETURNING FROM COTTON PICKING IN SOUTH CAROLINA
DURING RECONSTRUCTION.

it's all in the balance, it hasn't happened yet, it hasn't even begun yet but there is still time for it not to begin."

This fictional character's romantic escapism pales by comparison to the reality of Confederate revisionism. The Cult of the Lost Cause reworked the war to Southern advantage. "They may have won," the defeated South avowed, "but we remained gentlemen." This Lost Cause ideology became a kind of religion in the postbellum South, one that has been explored imaginatively by a growing body of historians. The slow and steady progress of hero worship and memorialization lifted the Stars and Bars of the Confederate battle flag out of the ashes and into a defiant stance. And the repercussions of this posture continue to the present day.

Post-surrender white Southerners recognized that they could re-build their region not just with bricks and mortar, but by laying a foun-dation for historical revisionism. To many, this involved reconfiguring facts to conform to political agendas. In the wake of Lee's surrender, former Confederates launched an immediate verbal and literary counter-attack. Curiously, many Northerners not only forgave former Confed-erates, granting them their historical license, but by the 1870s had joined the revisionist pack. When America's official Centennial festivities opened in Philadelphia in 1876, the theme of unification predominated.

Unlike their European and Latin American counterparts, former Confederate insurrectionists were not concerned with the possibility of

WOMEN'S ROLE IN GRAVE DECORATING WAS TO HONOR THE DEAD AND VALORIZE
THEIR POSITIONS AS HEARTH TENDERS.

CONFEDERATE MONUMENTS, SUCH AS THIS ONE NEAR HIGGINSVILLE, MISSOURI,
WERE TESTIMONY TO WOMEN'S FUNDRAISING TALENTS.

being beheaded, or even of prolonged imprisonment. Instead, some sought to recoup their losses at sword point by taking up the pen. In 1881 Jefferson Davis, former president of the Confederacy, published his own apologia, *The Rise and Fall of the Confederate Government*. By the last quarter of the century Southern voices had become cherished chroniclers of the "good old days," and by the turn of the century Southern historians exerted notable influence, even gaining positions within prestigious Ivy League institutions. None was more impressive than the prolific Ullrich Bonnell Phillips, writing from his position as a professor at Columbia University in New York City. The Phillips school of Southern history dominated the study of slavery for almost half a century after his publication of *American Negro Slavery* (1918). Phillips and his students preached a philosophy of planter paternalism, asserting that slavery was a benign institution—benevolent slave owners created a "plantation school," he suggested, to educate backward blacks to the virtues of discipline and productivity.

The images promoted by scholars and intellectuals were secondary, however, to the way in which the Old South, with its mass appeal to white Americans, was depicted within popular culture. Most strikingly, the immigrant generation that founded the American movie industry, along with their offspring (both literal and intellectual), became hooked on the tales and images of the Old South. Plantation epics supplanted historical texts while "moonlight and magnolia" captured the national imagination. Even if Americans did not learn most of their history from the silver screen between the world wars, and from the smaller screen, television, from the 1950s onward, the entertainment industry has indelibly fashioned nostalgic perceptions of the plantation South with these popular and sometimes purposefully misleading renditions,

---

Souvenirs demonstrate the continuing commercial appeal of *Gone With the Wind*'s legacy.

particularly those of the Civil War
era. At the same time serious treatment of slavery and its consequences has been extremely rare in
popular culture. Black artists and
critics rightfully deplore both the
sympathetic treatment of slaveholding and the lack of diversity in
depiction of the African-American
experience. Indeed, media com-
mentators have noted that in the
1990s, more black women have
been relegated to playing maids in
films and television programs than
ever before. And so we must ask
when will we see Harriet Tubman

on the screen, or Sojourner Truth? Harriet Jacobs or Susie King Taylor?
These celebrated figures of black resistance form significant counter-
legends to Lost Cause propaganda. African Americans rightly demand

---

ABOVE: ILLUSTRATION FROM A 1906 PUBLICATION, *DEM GOOD OLE TIMES*,
WHICH SENTIMENTALIZED THE DEATH OF A MAMMY, A STAPLE EPISODE
IN SOUTHERN MEMOIRS.
BELOW: A COMIC BOOK SERIES FROM THE 1980S.

JOANNE WHALLEY-KILMER AS SCARLETT AND ESTHER ROLLE AS MAMMY IN THE
1994 TELEVISION MINISERIES *SCARLETT*. THE DEATH OF MAMMY REMAINS LEGENDARY
SOUTHERN LORE, EVEN IN A 1990S VERSION.

more diverse illuminations of the past, not the comfortable cartoonish
aspects traditionally served up.

At a minimum, we must acknowledge that blacks within the Confederacy had a disproportionate stake in the outcome of the Civil War.
Black and white women on plantations were not left behind during
wartime, but were right at the center of their own victories and defeats.
As some have argued, the slaveholders' inability to maintain order, discipline, and productivity on slaveholding plantations was a major blow
to Confederate independence. Dislocations and deprivations plagued
white and black, rich and poor, and the plantations enjoyed little
respite from the ravages of war. Loss of household and loss of loved
ones all took their toll during the many long years of conflict. So the
drama of wartime struggle was not confined to combat in the field, but
included battles faced by the black and white women besieged on
Southern slaveholding estates, embittered and themselves locked in
struggle. Today, as well, the plantation remains contested terrain, a
vital intersection of historical images that summon up warring visions
of the southern past.

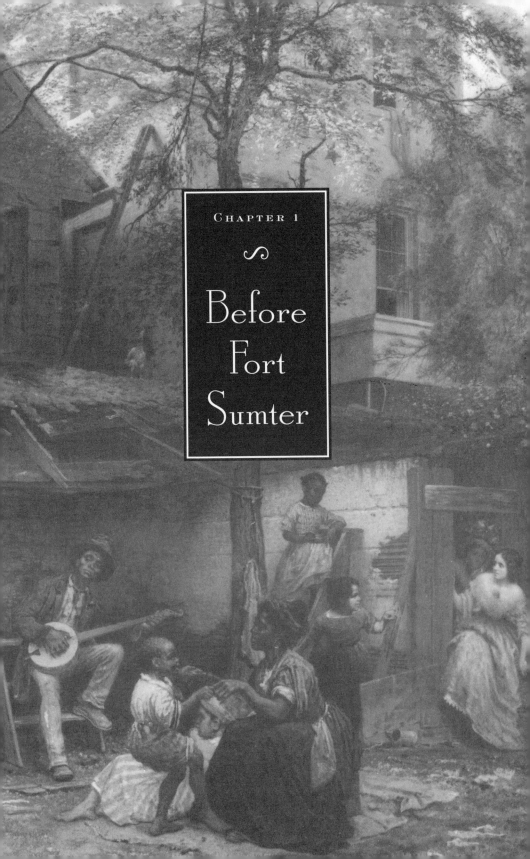

CHAPTER 1

Before Fort Sumter

Before
Fort Sumter

I n the antebellum South there were indeed belles and beaux and lavish entertainments. But there were also harsh epidemics, scorching heat, and hardscrabble living on the border. A complex interdependency developed between myth and reality, upcountry and low country, coastal and interior, urban and rural. Lush, conspicuous splendor was meant to hide the wrenching work necessary to maintain the grandiose estates that sprawled westward along with settlement. Slave owners hoped their pristine homes could in some way obscure the relentless filth and grind to which their human chattel were subjected in the building of the "cotton kingdom." Most white Southerners participated in this conspiracy, and all but a few knew that their role as co-conspirators was to conjure up a dream world—for Europeans only. It was a white man's fantasy, one that required bravado and delusion for full enjoyment.

With the early settlements of America's southern frontier through the middle of the seventeenth century, English promoters shamelessly hawked the South as a paradise on earth—a claim flatly contradicted by the realities of the first encounters. Sir Richard Grenville had led an expedition in 1584 that landed off the Carolina coast at Roanoke Island, and when he departed he left fifteen men behind to hold the fort. But when John White returned with a group of settlers in 1587, they found no survivors. White then sailed back to England, leaving behind his

---

own small band, which included his granddaughter, Virginia Dare, the first English child born in North America. But the Spanish Armada and other impediments delayed White's return to Roanoke, and when he landed in August 1590 the settlement had disappeared. This early group's sad fate, which has become a staple of Southern folklore, did not bode well.

And so propagandists went into high gear, with a literary outpouring that was nothing short of a crusade to convince Europeans that America was a glorious opportunity rather than a dangerous exile. British merchant Edward Bland wrote *The Discovery of New Britain* in 1651, advising readers to settle in the territory from thirty-five to thirty-seven degrees north latitude—well aware that Sir Walter Raleigh's *Morrow of History* located Eden along the thirty-fifth parallel north. Heaven, he claimed, could be found along a line that ran from Fayetteville, North Carolina, to Memphis, Tennessee (where Elvis Presley built his own paradise, Graceland).

An earlier generation of European explorers had criss-crossed the southern reaches of the continent in search of fountains of youth and cities of gold, but by the seventeenth century Europeans sought other treasures. They hoped to cultivate silkworms, grapes, orchards of olives, dates, lemons, and other exotic trees—in short, to turn America into a veritable Garden of Eden.

Despite the unrealistic dreams of merchants and patent holders,

THE SALE OF AFRICANS SUPPLIED WORKERS FOR THE LAND-RICH, LABOR-POOR SOUTH.

the South proved a surprising gold mine. White indentured servants came by the boatload with the hope of securing property and status once they had earned their freedom. Most whites who came as contract labor emerged as flourishing farmers within a decade. Some Virginians joined the ranks of men of influence in the House of Burgesses without having to wait even a generation for respectability and wealth. By the early eighteenth century the national resources of the American continent were mythic—from furs to crops, the New World seemed ripe for European plucking. The plantation legend was launched.

By the time of the American Revolution, Southern landowners, the majority of whom were descended from indentured servants, had produced a score of wealthy dynasties and several hundred lesser fortunes with the golden crop of tobacco. Robert "King" Carter and William Byrd were but two of the dozens of grandees who had ruled in Virginia in the first half of the eighteenth century. Farther south, Carolina low-country planters were cultivating the even more profitable crop of rice, as well as Sea Island cotton. Although the status of these colonial barons was mocked by the British, who nicknamed them "nabobs" (a corruption of the Hindi term for governor, *nawwab*), their wealth was the envy of the empire.

The transformation of the British colonies from wilderness to settlement to cultivation, especially in the plantation South, succeeded to a great extent because of the involvement of women. The earl of Southampton, concerned with the failing Virginia Company, argued that "the plantation can never flourish till families be planted and the respect of wives and children fix the people on the soil." The climate was harsh, many of the indigenous peoples were understandably hostile, and women faced grueling challenges. White women may not have been the initiators of expansion, but they were forced into full partnership in the building of the plantation South.

One of the most outstanding women of the South's early days was Eliza Lucas Pinckney. Born in the West Indies in 1722 and educated in England, she was a privileged child of a wealthy planter who moved his family to South Carolina in 1738. The next year, when her father was forced to return to Antigua to assume a royal appointment, the sixteen-year-old Eliza was left in charge of his three estates. She proved a talented manager of slave labor, successfully training slaves to cultivate indigo, which she imported from the West Indies in 1740. In 1744 she married widower Charles Pinckney and settled into the traditional role of plantation mistress and mother. The Pinckneys moved to London in

PLANTATION BURIAL (1860). NOTE THE PLANTER COUPLE NEARLY HIDDEN IN THE
RIGHT FOREGROUND AMONG THE TREES.

1753, but when their plantation began to fail in 1758 the couple returned to Carolina with a young daughter, leaving their two sons behind in school in England. Within six weeks of landing, Charles Pinckney died, and Eliza was once again forced to manage on her own. "I find it requires great care, attention and activity to attend properly to a Carolina Estate, tho' but a moderate one, to do one's duty and make it turn to account," she reported. "A variety of imployment gives my thoughts a relief from mellancholy subjects."

With the outbreak of the Revolutionary War, Pinckney devoted herself to her sons, who had returned from England and were actively involved in the colonial rebellion. In 1779 she was able to lend a large sum of plantation profits to the new state of South Carolina. At war's end her younger son, Thomas, was elected governor while his older brother, Charles, served as a delegate to the Constitutional Convention. Indeed, so great was Eliza Lucas Pinckney's contribution to the new country that after her death in 1793 George Washington asked to serve as one of her pallbearers in tribute to her devotion to the American cause.

Another Revolutionary foremother, Judith Giton Manigault, experienced even more of a dramatic struggle on her family's road to wealth and status. Giton and her husband, Huguenot refugees, fled France for South Carolina in 1685. When her husband died Giton remarried, this time wedding a distiller named Manigault. The couple acquired land, wealth, and political influence, but their successes were hard won.

"I have been six months without tasting bread, working like a ground slave; and have even passed three and four years without having food when I wanted it," Manigault recalled of her early years in Carolina.

Manigault's description reminds us that nearly all women in the early South were forced to perform arduous labor on the land. In the seventeenth-century South the majority of agricultural workers were white indentured servants, but by the eighteenth century planters used slaves. Indeed in 1722 Virginian Robert Beverly commented, "A white woman is rarely or never put to work in the ground, if she be good for anything else . . . whereas, on the other hand, it is a common thing to work a woman slave out of doors." Plantation fields were increasingly filled with the sons and daughters of Africa rather than the white laborers who might one day own the lands they had worked.

Slave women, imported in fewer number than men in the seventeenth and early eighteenth centuries, joined black men in the fields, shouldering equal burdens in the production of cotton and other cash crops. The slave population in the southern colonies (excluding Virginia) grew from only 600 in 1675 to over 180,000 a century later. And by that time the ratio of slave men to slave women was almost fifty-fifty. Public and private records reveal relatively little about African-American lives, although it is known that women were as eager for freedom as men. The American Revolution offered blacks a new opportunity along those lines, for the British granted emancipation to slaves of rebel masters when they fled to the redcoats. The plantation ledgers of many Revolutionary slaveholders are littered with complaints about slaves absconding—Thomas Jefferson lost twenty-three during the prolonged rebellion, including ten adult women and three girls. Over fifty slaves fled from John Ball's South Carolina plantation in 1780, including eighteen women, some with infants in arms. Charlotte, a slave woman, led away a handful on May 10, including "Betsy and her three children." A week later she returned to instigate a mass exodus: fifteen people, including three mothers with their children.

Approximately ten thousand slaves from the Savannah and Charleston region alone abandoned their masters during the Revolutionary War. One list of nearly three thousand slaves seeking British protection indicates that 43 percent were female, and that each mature woman traveled with an average of 1.5 children. The group was young, with 32 percent of them under age twenty and 17 percent under age ten. Fifty-seven percent of the runaway slave children were accompanied by their mothers only, 17 percent by both parents, 3 percent by fathers only,

and the rest by other relatives. Although many women risked their lives to escape a system that afforded so much oppression and so little opportunity, many runaway slaves like these found no real ease. Initially transported to the British Caribbean, they were then sent into exile in Nova Scotia and finally deported for resettlement in Africa.

Upon arrival in the American South, most African slaves were rapidly assimilated into the African-American community, learning English and converting to Christianity, for example. But many struggled to maintain a sense of themselves by retaining African names and customs. Despite the harsh coercive forces of slavery, which frequently worked against black pride and slave resistance, slave counterculture conveyed a sense of belonging, of kin and community. While slave

OPPOSITE: *THE GUARDIAN ANGEL*, AN ILLUSTRATION FROM EDWARD KING'S SKETCHES
OF THE SOUTH, WHICH RAN IN *SCRIBNER'S MAGAZINE* (1873–74).

owners drilled into slave children the creed that a master's power superseded parental authority, many slave mothers instilled in their families a value system that defied the master's dictates. Still, the facts of family life under slavery undermined even the strongest of values. All too many children became parentless as they were separated from their families to supply the southwestward migrations. In colonial Georgia children frequently were separated from parents by the age of six, and after the founding of the nation they were often shipped westward to newly organized territories and states. Nevertheless, many children deprived of their blood relatives developed deep and long-lasting relationships with "fictive kin"—aunts, uncles, or unrelated adults who stood in for departed parents. Furthermore, the slave population in general, deprived of traditional household patterns, embraced its young; orphaned of his or her birth parents, a child would nonetheless be "mothered" or "fathered" by the entire slave community.

Planters' greed as much as slaves' spiritual and emotional needs shaped the African-American family. Half of all slave marriages in which both spouses were still alive in 1865 had been broken up by masters; of those unions destroyed by sales, two-thirds had endured over five years and one in seven had lasted fifteen years or more. As for the marriages themselves, often slave owners permitted a slave to marry "abroad," to take a mate owned by another master. In other cases, however, owners tried to match up slaves on their own estate whom they considered suitable, with or without their consent. Sometimes a black preacher would offici-ate, or perhaps even a white clergyman would perform a ceremony—although a slave marriage had no standing before the law. Planters sometimes used the wedding as a means of rewarding loyal slaves, by lavishing them with food, flowers, and gifts. Brides might be supplied with wedding finery by approving mistresses.

Slaves celebrated their unions with or without white sanction, commonly observing the traditional African folk ceremony of jumping the broom. According to this rite, each couple jumped backward over a stick to mark the occasion, and whoever of the two accomplished the hop without mishap was predicted to rule the marriage. Tangled feet on the part of the groom provided a source of merriment, while hope and cheer—qualities in short supply in the slave community—flowed freely.

Pregnancies were times of stress as much as joy for a slave woman. Historical evidence shows that most young slave women abided by community codes that prohibited cohabitation before pair-bonding, which usually took place during the late teen years for women. There were few effective means of birth control, and children would follow shortly after marriage. Although slave babies were an important commodity for slave owners, there is little to suggest that owners gave expectant mothers much relief or reward. Many mothers-to-be might have pleaded for a respite from the harsh demands of fieldwork, but women rarely were excused from their labors. After giving birth, slave mothers toted their children to the field until they were weaned. During the British actress Fanny Kemble's visit to her husband's Georgia Sea Island plantation during the winter of 1838, she reported, "The women who visited me yesterday evening were all in the family-way, and came to entreat of me to have the sentence (what else can I call it?) modified which condemns them to resume their labor of hoeing in the fields three weeks after their confinement."

Such exertions did little to enhance the health of the mother or child. Although Kemble claimed that "the people on this plantation are well off, and consider themselves well off, in comparison with the slaves on some of the neighboring estates," she then went on to chronicle the women she had seen:

Fanny: six children, all dead but one
Nanny: three children, two dead
Leah: six children, three dead
Sophy: ten children, five dead
Sally: two miscarriages, three born, one dead
Charlotte: two miscarriages
Sarah: four miscarriages, seven born, five dead

Similar tales of woe were probably all too common for slave women on large estates throughout the South such as that of Pierce Butler, Kemble's husband, who was the second largest slave owner in Georgia.

AN ANONYMOUS SKETCH, *FEEDING TIME AT THE SLAVE CABINS*.

On large plantations an older slave might be designated to oversee a nursery where all infants and children were gathered—as many as fifty children from three months to eight years, the age when most slave offspring were expected to go to work in the fields. On smaller farms youngsters as young as seven were drafted into childcare, to supervise toddlers and others. Their diets and exercise varied dramatically, but little was done beyond preparing the young people for lives of drudgery.

Sundays were the single day of the week when slave families might be together, and on this free day many slave parents tended their own gardens. These gardens provided families with necessary food, and their care and cultivation were a means of survival rather than a luxury. The day off from fieldwork was crowded with essential chores. Wives also were burdened with laundry and cabin chores, making leisure an impossibility. Since the time and energies of the slave mother were absorbed with meeting the demands of her family as well as her owner's dictates, a slave woman's choices were considerably constrained.

Slavery created complex constellations of power in the antebellum South and even more convoluted family relations. The child of a slave mother and free father, for instance, was consigned to a life of slavery, while the child of a free mother and slave father (more common in the colonial period, but on the decline by the Revolution) was born free. The sexual double standard had a vicious twist within the plantation South, and it produced a peculiarly Southern dishonor. Illicit liaisons

THIS ANTEBELLUM WOODCUT, *FAMILY AMALGAMATION AMONG THE MEN-STEALERS*,
CONVEYS NORTHERN CONTEMPT FOR WHAT WAS CONSIDERED TO BE
SOUTHERN HYPOCRISY.

were condemned in the North under all circumstances, while the South
gave special dispensation to a white man involved with a black woman.
This category of affair was rarely tabulated on the register of moral
error in the antebellum South—unless the man flaunted his relationship with his black bedmate, or, worse yet, tried to legitimate the liaison
by marriage, which was outlawed in most Southern states.

Legitimation of these unions was relatively rare. Martin Van
Buren's vice president, Richard M. Johnson, scandalized his fellow
Southerners by publicly acknowledging his two daughters by a mulatto
concubine and marrying them off to white husbands. But it was Johnson's scorn of secrecy rather than his illicit biracial offspring that was at
issue. The existence of mixed-race children created a dilemma within
slaveholding society. Many planters who claimed that slaveholding was
a Christian system, one that brought heathens to God, were confronted
with the living evidence of some of slavery's sins—often by biracial offspring within their own households.

Within the repressed and contradiction-ridden South, race indelibly influenced patterns of sexual expression. Desire, impulse, and taboo
drove whites to entangle themselves with blacks from the colonial
period onward. By the nineteenth century slave owners were prepared
to countenance their economic exploitation of blacks for profit and
their sexual exploitation of blacks for pleasure.

One of the most powerful slave narratives of its day, Harriet Jacobs's *Incidents in the Life of a Slave Girl* (1861), written under the pseudonym of Linda Brent, illustrates the particular vulnerability of black women in the antebellum South. Born circa 1815, Jacobs grew up in the small town of Edenton, North Carolina, where her mistress taught her to read and write; her grandmother, a free black, also became a strong force in her early life. But when Jacobs's benevolent mistress died and she was willed to the family of Dr. James Norcom, a prominent physician, her life changed for the worse. In her extraordinary narrative Jacobs boldly confronts slaveholders' sexual brutality and the predicament she and other slave women faced. Her sensitive prose vividly paints her dilemma: "I now entered on my fifteenth year—a sad epoch in the life of a slave girl. My master began to whisper foul words in my ear. Young as I was, I could not remain ignorant

of their import. I turned from him with disgust and hatred. But he was my master. I was compelled to live under the same roof with him." Jacobs's tale is a stirring saga, and her escape from her master, her attempts to emancipate her two children (by another white man), and her years in hiding are riveting reading.

Fanny Kemble witnessed slave women's vulnerability when she recorded the plight of her husband's bondwoman, Judy, raped by the overseer: "Mr. K[ing] forced her, flogged her severely for having resisted him and then sent her off, as a farther punishment, to Five Pound—a horrible swamp in a remote corner of the estate, to which the slaves are sometimes banished for such offenses as are not sufficiently atoned for by the lash." These horrors were compounded when Judy gave birth to King's child, in response to which King's wife whipped her and sent her back to Five Pound. The endless terrors of plantation life reverberate in these infrequently documented but compelling accounts of sexual brutality.

Above: A young, mixed-race female slave was considered a valuable prize. Women slaves were often considered to be commodities for sexual exploitation in the Old South marketplace.

In stark contrast, white men exalted white women's purity, keeping them on the pedestal while consigning black women to the auction block. The plantation mistress, expected to turn a blind eye to men's sexual activity across the color line, rarely retaliated. But in an isolated and terrible example of what vengeance she might wreak if she stepped off her pedestal, one jealous wife, a slave reported, "slipped in a colored gal's room and cut her baby's head clean off 'cause it belonged to her husband." Despite the horrors and destabilization such liaisons created within plantation society, slavery flourished nonetheless. This powerful system was the backbone of the antebellum Southern economy, and women rarely fought it.

Many plantation mistresses were unprepared for both the increasing burdens and the new responsibilities thrust upon them as the Southern economy grew in response to changes wrought by the industrial revolution and the westward expansion of the United States. With the invention of the cotton gin in 1793, the southwest land grab began and the plantation South greedily extended its reach across the continent. Planters exported cotton at unprecedented rates and with the cry for cotton, the demand for slaves seemed limitless. After the end of the external slave trade in 1807, Southerners were dependent upon natural increase to supply slaves to the young white men seeking their fortunes. Only smuggling and selling African-American children provided new slave labor for the agriculturally rich regions of the Mississippi Delta and the Black Belt (a large swath of fertile land stretching across central

ABOVE: AN ETCHING, *LADIES WHIPPING GIRLS*, DEMONSTRATES ABOLITIONIST IRE AT CRUELTY FOSTERED BY THE "PECULIAR INSTITUTION."

THIS GRINNING PORTRAIT OF AN ENSLAVED GIRL, TITLED *MISS JIM-IMA CROW*,
CHARACTERIZES THE POPULAR IMAGE OF AFRICAN AMERICANS AS "HAPPY DARKIES."

Elizabeth Taylor in a scene from *Raintree County* (1957), reflecting the stereotypical image of pampered belles in films depicting the Old South.

Alabama and Mississippi named for its rich black soil). The cotton revolution stimulated the settlement of western Georgia, Alabama, Mississippi, and northern Louisiana.

The increasing dependence on slave labor by Southern landowners placed growing demands on the planter's wife. And the management of estates, in which women were often deeply involved, became more complex and burdensome throughout the first half of the nineteenth century. The plantation mistress was expected to provide for her husband's slaves in four important areas: food, clothing, shelter, and medical care. The plantation mistress might have seemed mere decoration, but she was the living symbol of her civilization and the linchpin for gaining a foothold in the southwestern wilds.

The image of the plantation mistress was a carefully cultivated distortion of reality meant to embody the grace and ease to which white Southerners aspired. Of course the majority of white women in the South were far removed from the leisure afforded on grand estates. Fewer than twenty-five hundred families in the region (out of a white population of three million) constituted the planter elite, and even those women whose husbands possessed great wealth were not the portraits of luxury described in legend.

Only a small percentage of plantations employed overseers, most often because the owners were absent. On residential plantations, the mistress undertook much more than running the household for her own family. She was expected to manage a range of arduous tasks: growing herbs, planting gardens, blending medicines, dipping candles, spinning thread, weaving cloth, knitting socks, sewing clothes, supervising the slaughter of hogs, processing and curing meats, scouring cooper utensils, preserving vegetables, and churning butter.

Just as Southern planter statesmen often compared themselves to Roman senators, so too did their wives find in the Roman matron a cultural ideal. Responsibilities and restrictions for the matron in the Old South were modeled on those in classical Rome. J.P.V.D. Balsdon described the Roman matron: "While the husband took care of the land, his wife took care of the household. She held the keys of the store cupboard, she brought up the children. The larger the establishment, the greater the number of slaves, both in the house and on the land. . . . She never joined the guests after a meal until she had seen the silver locked up and given the slaves their supper."

This maternalistic ideal was adopted by the Southern elite as well. But while white women were expected to take on all these roles with noble resignation, in private many filled letters and diaries with litanies of complaint. Susan Dabney Smedes recalled in her postwar memoir, "The mistress of a plantation was the most complete slave on it." Setting aside the utter absurdity of such a claim, it is important to stress that mistresses themselves believed this maxim before and after the Civil War. This lament stemmed in part from the monumental clash of myth and reality experienced by most white women. The role of "the lady" met the needs of a chauvinist stereotype, while the practical

A PLANTATION MISTRESS AND SLAVE AS VIEWED BY AN ANTEBELLUM WATERCOLORIST.

concerns of everyday life on the plantation created a decidedly different set of demands.

Planter-class women recognized the financial and legal disabilities imposed by gender, and most accepted these limitations as unalterable. Women did not resist so much as resent their dependency. The plantation mistress found herself trapped within a system over which she had little control, one from which she felt she had no means of escape. Women did not inhabit mythical estates but lived instead on productive working plantations where routines were grueling. Cotton was king, white men ruled, and both white women and slaves served the same master.

Planter daughters married at a young age: the average age of plantation brides was twenty, while northern brides married at twenty-four. Southern grooms, however, married at twenty-eight. Slave women found their mates at younger ages, usually marrying by their late teens. But while slave women made the transition to married life fairly smoothly, often remaining within their immediate community and maintaining familiar bonds, the transformation for white women from belle to matron could be abrupt and disconcerting.

One day a young white woman might be the pampered daughter

OPPOSITE: A PORTRAIT OF MR. AND MRS. JAMES BEATY OF MISSISSIPPI CAPTURES
THE WEALTH AND STATUS OF PLANTERS ON THE EVE OF THE CIVIL WAR.

of a planter family, free of responsibility, a carefree schoolgirl pursuing fashion and romance. But marriage would change all that. In short order she could be torn from the bosom of her family and anchored on an isolated plantation, saddled with her own household and charged with the care and feeding of her husband's slaves. It was a fate for which many if not most brides were wholly unprepared. One planter wrote to his daughter: "It is a fault in female education housekeeping is not made more a part of it; book learning is not sufficient: the kitchen and dairy must be attended to as well as the drawing room."

One new bride confided that she was overwhelmed when she realized "for the first time the responsibilities of the mistress on a large plantation and of the nights of sorrow and tears these thoughts had given her." The despair could age women dramatically. In 1831 a woman wrote of her transformation: "Now I have turned housekeeper for to my sorrow I know there is no romance in going from the smoke house to the store room and from there to the cellar half a dozen times a day." The sobering experience of housekeeping was offset by the joy many women found in starting their own families. Yet childbearing, too, entailed new and sometimes daunting responsibilities.

Health was generally poor in the South, with mortality rates running twice as high in the Deep South as in the North. Death in childbirth and infant mortality combined to instill a healthy fear of pregnancy among Southern women. Cholera, yellow fever, and influenza were also common killers in the antebellum era. The burdens of family health and the nursing of slaves were consistently the lot of plantation mistresses. The few women who escaped these duties were themselves invalids— indeed for many women of the plantocracy, the only means of survival was retreat, and some took to their couches rather than face the crushing demands on slaveholding estates.

Many plantation mistresses recognized that they lived within a culture

that reinforced male power. Although most women valued family, kin, and companionship, even the wealthiest of planter wives spent most of their lives in isolation on remote estates scattered throughout the South. The plantation mistress, most often the only white woman on the estate, was denied almost any society. Exaggerated chaperonage prevented planter women access to travel. Even adult white women were prohibited from excursions off the plantation without white male escorts.

One melancholy Southerner, Maria Campbell, the wife of Virginia Governor David Campbell, wrote to her husband in Richmond in 1822, bemoaning his absence during the Christmas holidays. Attempting to comfort her, he replied: "For whatever you may think of the lonesomeness of your situation—I can assure you mine is much more so. The company here affords some amusement for a few days, but its novelty is soon gone—and then, to me, there is no more pleasure in it, without you, than if I were in a solitary wilderness." Reluctant to cede the point, his wife responded: "You have it in your power to enjoy company when you please. . . . But here I am shut up like a canary bird (in my dear little cot, to be sure) without the power of obtaining society." In his next letter, her husband agreed, but concluded, "I know you are shut up like the canary bird, but you sing so sweetly that to make you sing seems mere justification for the tyranny exercised."

This metaphorical imprisonment created real suffering, but the disadvantage paled considerably in contrast with the lives of the other women on the plantation—female slaves. Their shackles and chains were not symbolic, but true restraints that sometimes included physical confinement, depriving them of mobility or choice, and locking them within a system that all too often separated them from kin.

The impact of slavery, however, was not limited to planters and slaves, the two groups most directly implicated in the institution. True, the dynamics of slavery excluded most people in the South—the non-slaveholding white majority. But whites denied the privileges of the planter class—the rites of exploitation and the fruits of planter wealth—gained status despite their exclusion by their position on a mythological Southern social hierarchy that deemed even rich and refined blacks inferior to the most degraded whites. They were spared the cultural dishonor reserved for all people of color: the label of "mudsill" and the stigma of absolute inferiority. The plantocracy undermined class conflict by enforcing rigid color lines and exalting white superiority. During harvest festivals and on court day, at church

MOST WHITE SOUTHERN WOMEN, EVEN THE MAJORITY OF SLAVEOWNERS' WIVES,
TYPICALLY DID NOT LIVE ON PLANTATIONS, RATHER IN MORE MODEST RESIDENCES.

and during elections, the white classes mingled. Finally, even the lowliest white "crackers" could claim a badge of status within Southern society—the color of their skin.

Within the South a small group of whites controlled the destiny of the vast majority of blacks, and bound the interests of the white yeoman class to their own. Large planters established elaborate systems of patronage to ensure the loyalty of local farmers. Often a planter, who might own the only cotton gin in the county, would lend the equipment to neighboring small farms and then send along the neighbors' cotton bales with his own to his broker, or provide other perks. Sometimes an overseer might be hired, the son of a neighbor, off an adjoining farm, or a young man without land given his first slave as payment for services rendered—a leg up into a system in which his employer was heavily invested. A planter father with too many offspring and not enough land might marry off a daughter to a local landowner, with a dowry of slaves to speed the couple's climb up the economic ladder. Slave owners often paid the struggling sons of neighbors to serve as patrollers, enforcing the slave pass system that was meant to keep African Americans in their place.

These situations and others knit together the white South, already

the most homogeneous population within the country. In reality the vast majority of white Southerners would never be slave owners and those who might come to own slaves would rarely rise to the rank of planter. Despite this fundamental split in economic interests, however, many white Southerners rallied to the cause of slavery and reviled Yankee interference. Ironically, those who seemed most committed to defending the honor of this system were often drawn from the *nouveau riche* among slave owners. James Henry Hammond, the South Carolina senator who popularized the slogan "cotton is king," was born the son of a schoolteacher but gained his vast fortune the old-fashioned way—by marrying a planter heiress. He and others like him subscribed to the theory that slavery was a dynamic, open system that allowed any white man to gamble and work his stake into a fiefdom.

Thrown into this bubbling cauldron of color, class, gender, and status, the growing sectional conflict considerably spiced the brew. The way the behavior of Yankee entrepreneurs—manipulating the cotton market and denying blacks employment in cotton mills—contradicted the antislavery they preached inflamed Southern statesmen. From the Missouri crisis in 1819, when Congress reached a legislative settlement that required all new states north of 36° 30′ north latitude to join the nation as free states while all below would be slave, to the Dred Scott decision in 1857 in which the Supreme Court upheld the constitutional-

SOUTH CAROLINA TOPSEY IN A FIX.

ity of slavery throughout the nation, political and legal differences were
papered over by a steady stream of compromises. Violence threatened
the nation, and statesmen declared the strain between North and South
to be an "irrepressible conflict."

The threat of abolitionists was scorned and ridiculed in the South
until the antislavery zealot John Brown and his band of followers
seized an arsenal at Harpers Ferry, Virginia, in 1859, hoping to stir
up slave insurrections. This attack alerted all "fire-eaters"—as ardent
Southern sectionalists were called—that actions would speak louder
than words. Even Brown's hanging failed to quench the Southern thirst
for revenge. The following year, a spirited and fracturing presidential
campaign caused even more unrest as four major candidates sought
to occupy the White House. When Abraham Lincoln was elected, a
Republican identified with a platform for "Free Soil, Free Labor, Free
Men," strident Southern politicos, most especially those South Carolinians who preached the doctrine of states rights, argued that they
could no longer stand with the North. Secession was advocated as a
peaceable solution, in hopes that the South might stand apart.

And so, in December 1860, South Carolinians met in Charleston to
declare their independence. Many hoped other states would jump on
the secession bandwagon, and indeed by February seven states, all in

THE BATTLE OF FORT SUMTER AS DEPICTED IN AN ISSUE OF *HARPER'S WEEKLY*.

the Deep South, had followed suit to form the Confederate States of America. With the Confederacy's firing on Fort Sumter in April 1861 and Lincoln's call to arms, four more states, including Virginia, joined the rebellion rather than take up arms against fellow Southerners. By now, the rebellion clearly meant war.

The martial spirit was an integral part of Southern culture. More white Southerners were trained with arms, enrolled in local guards, and were generally better prepared to fight than their northern counterparts. Southerners were disproportionately represented at West Point and in the United States Army. But while Virginian Robert E. Lee, the commander in charge of apprehending John Brown during his Harpers Ferry attack, was consumed with regret at the thought of turning his guns against former classmates and comrades, his lot was cast with the Confederacy.

Stories of brother against brother have long been told, but the stories of women's critical roles in the war effort, and even those stories of sister against sister, still await a larger audience. Before the outbreak of battle, women, too, shared in the dream of peaceable separation. But the guns erupting on Charleston's battery at Fort Sumter that April weekend in 1861 shattered illusions. The patriotic crush to raise a Confederate army stampeded any hopes of peaceful resolution, without bloodshed. The veil was ripped off, and even the sweetness of victory on July 21, 1861, at the first battle of Manassas (known in the North as Bull Run) could not diminish the anxieties that swept across the plantation South.

What might happen when men went marching off to war? How would women and children survive the dangers and damage of a civil conflict? The courage white Southern men wasted on boasting might well be spent by the time they encountered their well-equipped enemy. The romance of war, in all its hypothetical splendor, vanished with the first flow of blood, and the nation was transfigured in the cloud of smoke over Charleston Bay. As the women who watched on rooftops knew, and as their mothers, sisters, and the slaves anchored on plantations would soon discover, their world would never be the same.

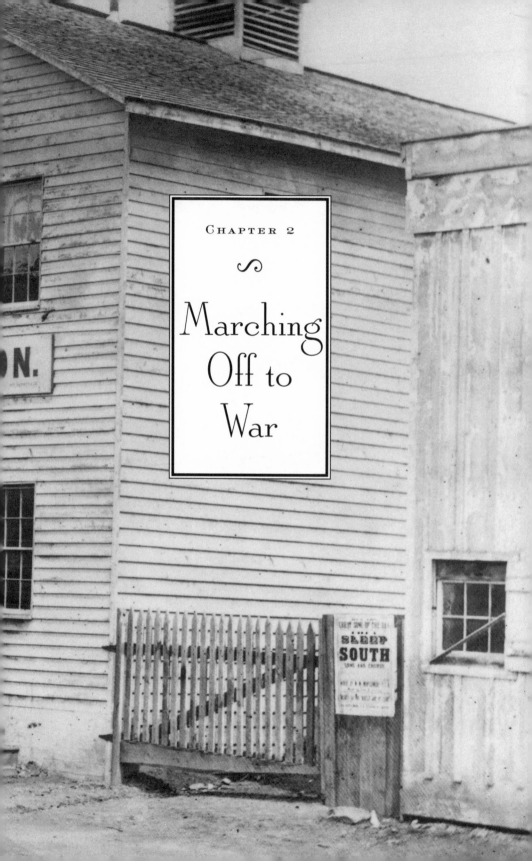

CHAPTER 2

Marching
Off to
War

Marching Off to War

T he Civil War became the great divide for Americans. Blurred passions shaped the life and death decisions that tore families as well as the nation apart. The call to arms created overnight transformations—from civilians into soldiers, from neighbors into enemies, from hearthside into home front. People and territories were thrown into terrible conflict with little or no time to adjust to the wrenching changes.

Secession created unique problems. One state even split apart during the rebellion, the northwestern corner of Virginia siding with the Union as West Virginia, while most of the citizenry, along with the anguished Robert E. Lee, joined the Confederacy. Some states were embattled throughout, like Missouri, which was ruled by two competing governments during wartime.

Planter men and women were torn over the question of the war's inevitability. One matron in Liberty County, Georgia, wrote in 1860 with supreme confidence, "I cannot see a shadow of reason for civil war in the event of Southern Confederacy." Nevertheless the shrewder Mary Boykin Chesnut, the wife of a South Carolina senator, saw the handwriting on the wall: "These foolish, rash, hare-brained Southern lads . . . are thrilling with fiery ardor. The red-hot Southern martial spirit is in the air."

From Abraham Lincoln's election onward secession fever was in

THIS NORTHERN PORTRAIT OF SOUTHERN WOMEN URGING THEIR MEN ON TO WAR
APPEARED IN *FRANK LESLIE'S ILLUSTRATED* IN 1863.

the air. Once South Carolina broke with the Union and the Confederacy was formed, Southerners were caught up in the heat of politics. On
February 26, 1861, Virginian Mary Lou Reid wrote to her father,
Samuel, about the Washington's birthday celebrations, "The Question
under discussion was 'whether Virginia should unite with the Cotton
States of a central Confederacy.'" Debates fired up across the South, in
taverns and parlors, from pulpits to courthouse steps.

This heady atmosphere was well captured in Margaret Mitchell's
epic novel *Gone With the Wind*. In one of the opening scenes, gentlemen

discuss the sectional split on an April afternoon while ladies nap upstairs. The boasting builds to a ludicrous crescendo: "'Of course we'll fight'—'Yankee thieves'—'We could lick them in a month'—'Why, one Southerner can lick twenty Yankees'—'Teach them a lesson they won't soon forget'—'Peaceably? they won't let us go in peace'—'They want war; we'll make them sick of war.'" Rhett Butler's unwelcome attempt to deflate the balloon of self-delusion, which expands as the afternoon wears on, fails miserably.

In 1790 Southern patriarch Thomas Jefferson had warned his newly married daughter Patsy: "The happiness of your life depends now on continuing to please a single person. To this all other objects must be secondary; even your love for me, were it possible that it could ever be an obstacle." Jefferson had watched his country form in the painful upheaval of revolution and had witnessed families torn apart by divided loyalties. Now his grandchildren's generation was confronting this same dilemma. In August 1861, Mississippi matron Jane Pickett contemplated crowds of Confederates cheering on soldiers bound for

AFRICAN AMERICANS RARELY APPEARED IN THE THOUSANDS OF PHOTOGRAPHS TAKEN IN UNION CAMPS, BUT WERE ALMOST ALWAYS POSED WITH WHITES, INVARIABLY IN KNEELING OR SITTING POSITIONS TO "FRAME" THE PRINCIPAL SUBJECTS.

Richmond, and battle, and remarked on an "enthusiasm which had not been witnessed, perhaps, since the days of the Revolution in '76. It was touching to see old men and women who witnessed the birth of our Republic now weeping over its downfall; and at their side a tiny grand-child waving its hat with unconscious smiles of glee."

Southern gentlemen, young men especially, were propelled by patriotism into military service. Women's roles in this unfolding drama were less clear-cut. In general they stood by their men during the painful decisions made in the spring of 1861. Mary Todd Lincoln strongly supported the Union cause, despite the fact that she feared for her son, Robert, who eventually served under Ulysses S. Grant. At the same time the First Lady masked her inner turmoil as three of her step-brothers joined the Confederate army. The dilemma in the White House was echoed in homes throughout the country. Confederate matron Septima M. Collis reported in her memoir, "I never fully real-ized the fratricidal character of the conflict until I lost my idolized brother Dave of the Southern army one day, and was nursing my Northern husband back to life the next." President Lincoln's Southern relations were accorded suspicious treatment. Elodie Todd, the First Lady's half sister who resided in Selma, Alabama, when war broke out, complained to her fiancé, "I never go in Public that my feelings are not wounded." Perhaps because of her connection to the hated Lincoln, Elodie Todd became a visible and vocal participant in secessionist cere-monies. National press attention focused on her presentation of a silken banner to the Magnolia Cadets, a local unit manned entirely by Ala-bama gentry that was formed to counter the image of the conflict as a rich man's war and a poor man's fight. Although Todd's fiancé was the company commander, she still remained Lincoln's sister-in-law, so despite her marriage she was plagued throughout the war.

Theodore Roosevelt recalled that as a young boy in New York City, one of his favorite nursery games was "blockade running." While his father was out recruiting support for the Union army, his mother and her Southern kin living in Manhattan felt trapped behind enemy lines, forced into silence during dinner table talk but not idly sitting by. Young Roosevelt remembered his mother's assignations in Central Park, where food and medical supplies were donated to smugglers who could direct goods to his maternal kin in Georgia or to other places it was needed behind Confederate lines.

When war broke out, slave owner Pierce Butler, living in Philadel-phia, became alarmed about the safety of his extensive holdings in

Georgia and tried to travel South. Detained and arrested in August 1861, Butler was charged with treason and held in jail for two months. His two daughters, the offspring of his broken marriage to Fanny Kemble, were severely distraught over their father's confinement, but suffered divided loyalties. Butler's older daughter, Sarah, like her mother, was a confirmed abolitionist who supported the Union cause. She was active in the Sanitary Commission and worked for Confederate defeat. Her only sibling, Fanny, however, sided against the Union and presumably with her father. After the war, Butler and his younger daughter moved South. Fanny's devotion to Dixie, where she settled permanently following her father's death in 1867 and attempted to revive the family's Sea Island estates, grew in spite of the fact that she had spent her life in Pennsylvania, Massachusetts, and abroad, with the exception of a few childhood months on the Butler plantations. Hundreds upon thousand of families were equally torn apart when a civil war overtook them.

In the South, Confederate loyalty was not only the duty of white women but a weapon the state wanted to brandish to bring straggling men into patriotic service. One Selma belle broke her engagement because her fiancé did not enlist before their proposed wedding day. Instead of marrying him, she sent her abandoned bridegroom a skirt and female undergarments, advising him, "Wear these or volunteer." Virginia patriot Judith Brockenbrough McGuire confessed, "Almost every girl plaits her own hat, and that of her father, brother, and lover, if she has the bad taste to have a lover out of the army, which no girl of spirit would do unless he is incapacitated by sickness or wounds." This kind of rhetoric enforced a loyalty that crushed dissent.

Public support for the war created a strange mix of

THIS PORTRAIT OF A CONFEDERATE MOTHER AND CHILD WAS TAKEN FOR A SOLDIER TO CARRY OFF TO WAR.

AN UNWELCOME RETURN.

THREE MONTHS' VOLUNTEER. "What! don't you know me—your own husband?"
DAUGHTER OF COLUMBIA. "Get away! No husband of mine would be here while the country needs his help."

symbols and images. On the one hand, Confederate manhood demanded separation from the precious home and loved ones men pledged to protect. White men's enlistment in military service might rob the household of its irreplaceable male icon, the slaveowner patriarch. Yet it was a woman's duty to deny men any choice. With love of newly formed country elevated above all else, matriarchs assumed the role of the virtuous conscience. While Southern honor required that the petty concerns of individuals be suborned by the state, this was nothing new. Yet the South prided itself on its white woman's zealotry, with the press promoting stories of female vigilance in the face of male reluctance.

North Carolina's *Raleigh Register* reported just such an incident in September 1863: "A young lady was engaged to be married to a soldier in the army. The soldier suddenly returned home. 'Why have you left the army?' she inquired of him. 'I have found a substitute,' he replied. 'Well, sir, I can follow your example, and find a substitute, too. Good Morning.' And she left him in the middle of the room, a disgraced soldier." These cautionary tales, meant to reinforce the duty of both men and women to set aside personal concerns for the good of the cause, were as abundant in the North as in the South at war's beginning.

ABOVE: THIS CARTOON EMPHASIZES WOMEN'S ROLES IN ENFORCING PATRIOTIC FERVOR.

Didactic stories appeared with increasing frequency in the fall of 1862 and throughout 1863 as the painful realities of war sunk in. The draft riots in New York City in July 1863 demonstrated the waning enthusiasm for wartime military service. In the South, poor harvests and shrinking supplies hit the region's farms hard. Men in gray wanted to protect their families from starvation as well as invading Yankees, but Confederate folklore warned of dire consequences. In one piece of journalistic melodrama, a complaining wife is widowed as a result of placing her own selfish concerns over those of her country. In March 1863 Alabama's *Selma Reporter* printed "A Solemn Warning to Wives," in which a wife, in a letter to her spouse in the Confederate army "magnified her troubles and the suffering and earnestly entreated her husband to return home." This cheerless plea led him to become "restless, discontented, unhappy," and, as a result, he deserted. Apprehended, the soldier was tried and executed, leaving his wife "haunted with the thought that her exaggerated representations of her trials and sufferings caused her husband's death." The Dixie correspondent found a moral in this tragedy: "Let this case be a lesson to all wives and mothers. When you write to soldiers, speak words of encouragement; cheer their hearts, fire their souls, and arouse their patriotism. Say nothing that will embitter their thoughts or swerve them from the path of patriotic duty."

The message was constant and consistent: white women must rally their men to the Confederate cause, hammering home the necessity of the fight. Men might falter, but the ladies of the South must be the bedrock upon which the new nation could be built. Despite women's presumed "softer natures" and Christian principles, Confederate propaganda remodeled the feminine ideal into the "iron magnolia"—a portrait retinted and distorted by Yankee propaganda and christened the "rebel spitfire."

In the North, Southern white women were venomously lampooned as the true warmongers of the Confederacy, Eves goading their men for the fall. The Northern press ridiculed what they saw as the savage appetite of Confederate women for secession and bloodshed. Cartoons satirized plantation mistresses and portrayed their patriotism with gallows humor. The harsh images were reminiscent of women knitting at the foot of the guillotine during the French Revolution. Attacks upon Southern ladies were meant to throw chivalrous men in gray off balance, unhinging the delicately balanced scaffolding that underpinned gender convention during wartime.

The Southern press, of course, painted the support of its "ladies" in quite a different light. Women's duties were showcased in traditionally feminine terms despite the masculine domain of war. In 1863 *Southern Field and Fireside* boasted of women's influence, and wondered how the war effort would fare without it: "Can you imagine what would be the moral condition of the Confederate army in six months?" Instead of becoming "cut-throat and vagabond," the Southern soldier was guaranteed to remain "a gentleman of honor, courage, virtue and truth," all through feminine influence. While Clara Barton, who organized Union

NORTHERN CARTOON LABELED *SECESH INDUSTRY*. ONE SOUTHERN WOMAN'S DIARY CONFIRMED REPORTS OF A CONFEDERATE WOMAN KEEPING A YANKEE SKULL ON HER DRESSING TABLE.

women into a nursing corps, envisioned her role as "a bit in the mouth, the curb on the neck of the war horse," Confederate ladies, by contrast, were portrayed as enthusiastic wielders of riding crops, whipping men into a frenzy for victory.

The war brought out contradictory and chaotic notions of gender conventions for whites. Confederate ideologues counted on ladies' willingness to stand behind the war effort with both moral and material support. But while some planters' wives might embrace this more aggressive role, many collapsed under the burdens it imposed. Confederate diarist Fannie Beers confided that although one mother "kept up splendid until after [her son] got off," once he left for the army, she was unable to "get over it." Beers and others tried to channel women's energies into patriotic war work. Women felled by grief could not simply withdraw until loved ones returned, but must plunge into service. Patriotism demanded women's total compliance with the war machine, and so most white wives and mothers donned masks of stoic endurance, fighting off fears that might cripple or paralyze wartime plantations.

Wounded. This dramatic image reflects the very real scenes of drama that followed the posting of death and casualty lists after each battle.

Southern women were promised that their courage and spirit would enable the men to emerge victorious. Many saw this as a sacred duty. One Georgian advised her countrywomen to "hurl the destructive novel in the fire and turn our poodles out of doors, and convert our pianos into spinning wheels. . . . I feel a new life within me, and my ambition aims at nothing higher than to become an ingenious, economical, industrious housekeeper, and an independent Southern woman." Confederate ladies subscribed to the popular cultural prescription that while women's efforts alone would not win the war, without them the war could not be won.

The wives of soldiers were taxed severely by the emotional demands of war. Alabama bride Mary Williamson wept for weeks before her husband joined the army, always confining her crying sessions to solitary moments. But when he finally departed she confessed to her diary, "This great sorrow makes me forget I ever had such a feeling as patriotism." Williamson and others felt cheated by the firebrands who had predicted the war wouldn't last the summer and that the Yankees would be easily licked. "It seems this war is destined to last a long time," she lamented. "I had no idea it would ever result this seriously."

Naïveté is a common thread in the private writings of women during this period. Georgia schoolgirl Augusta Kollock wrote to her brother at the Virginia Military Institute in January 1861 to report blithely about secession, discussing the formation of such local companies as the Savannah Rifles, the Blue Caps, and the Rattlesnakes. Kollock wrote that if war was declared she believed their father would join up. She complained about the federal government, and warned, "they may have to exterminate us." This ghoulish claim is made in jest by a poor child who could little imagine the devastation a scorched earth policy would wreak on her home state in the years to come.

Secessionists gathered in Montgomery, Alabama, to form the new Confederate government on February 18, 1861. There they inaugurated President Jefferson Davis (a former Mississippi senator) and Vice President Alexander Hamilton Stephens (a former Georgia delegate to the House of Representatives). Most who attended were festive and gay. Alabamian Eleanor Noyes Jackson reported the occasion to her sister: "The ladies trimmed Estelle Hall beautifully. Oh! the crowd, and such a one. The greatest variety of costume you can imagine. People from town, people from country, young and old . . . every house, little and big, was illuminated from the capitol to the exchange. . . . In short, yesterday was a great day for Montgomery."

Many plantation mistresses throughout the South saw the Confederacy as a means of reconstructing the political hierarchy, reconfiguring social constellations, and claiming new status. Too few comprehended the price this ceremony would extract from its people. Certainly women in Charleston were less able to take matters lightly after witnessing the Confederate army firing on Fort Sumter. Although no soldiers died during the battle (the only death came accidentally, after the white flag), the spectacle of bombardment impressed and shook observers. A young girl in Charleston, Emma Holmes, confided in her diary on Saturday, April 13, 1861: "All yesterday evening and during the night our battering continued to fire at regular intervals. . . . The scene at Fort Sumter must have been awful beyond description." She went on to report excitement, flag-waving, and cheering, but still a faint shiver of fear is mixed with the gaiety.

Mary Custis Lee, the wife of Robert E. Lee, was pained by Virginia's secession and her husband's resignation of his commission as field commander of the United States army. Martha Washington's

THE INAUGURATION OF JEFFERSON DAVIS, FORMER SENATOR FROM MISSISSIPPI, IN FEBRUARY 1861. DAVIS WAS THE CONFEDERATE STATES OF AMERICA'S FIRST AND ONLY PRESIDENT.

THE CONFEDERATE WHITE HOUSE, RICHMOND, VIRGINIA.

great-granddaughter, she took pride in her family's heritage. On the day of her husband's decision to join the Confederacy she wrote to one of her seven children: "With a sad heavy heart, my dear child, I write, for the prospects before us are sad indeed as I think both parties are wrong in this fratricidal war, there is nothing comforting even in the hopes that God may prosper the right, for I see no *right* in the matter. We can only pray that in his mercy he will spare us." Mary Custis Lee's despair was confined to her private correspondence, for a Virginia matron reported a few weeks later: "Mrs. General Lee has been with us for several days. She is on her way to the lower country, and feels that she has left Arlington for an indefinite period. They removed their valuables, silver, etc., but the furniture is left behind. I never saw her more cheerful, and she seems to have no doubt of our success. We are looking to her husband as our leader with implicit confidence." The cheerful appearances of Confederate wives inspired and protected, in some measure, this confidence.

But innocent bravado rarely survived the first casualties. Mary Boykin Chesnut confronted war with the death of her friend, a Colonel Bartow of Georgia in July 1861. And when the full report of the first battle of Bull Run arrived, Chesnut was reduced to "the most dreary

state at the loss of so many friends." As with most women of the plantocracy, the war became real only for Chesnut when the funerals commenced. The prolonged agonies of the wounded and the final farewells
of burial weighed heavily on the women left behind. Tending to the
messy debris of combat was "women's work," part of the harsh reality
of the home front. Whether the battle resulted in victory or defeat, the
bodies had to be counted, the dead buried, the families notified.

The first summer of war was a relatively glorious season for the
Confederacy. Mississippi plantation mistress Jane Pickett recounted the
vibrant atmosphere of Richmond, the Confederate capital, during this
honeymoon era:

> Companies in dress parade marching, horsemen riding to and fro,
> reminded me of thrilling scenes around the Alhambra or I should
> say the ill-fated Granada. But that was not the destiny of our be-
> loved Richmond the splendid battles at Bull Run and Manassas of
> the 18th and 21st have fully been proven. The "Grand Army" of
> the Hessians! Thought to cross the Potomac, have a little brush
> with the Rebels and wind up with a magnificent ball at night in
> Richmond. . . . But the "ball" wound up too soon for them, and in
> a way they did not expect. The [Yankee] women had ball dresses
> with them, & baby carriages; Silver plate for the Saturnalia, pipes of
> the choicest wines for their bacchanals, 32,000 sets of handcuffs
> for their prisoners. . . . Such a complete rout of an enemy was
> never before seen; it is said by an eyewitness to be a page lost to
> history, for it never can be described.

However, by the fall of 1861 the tenor of Confederate women's letters began to change, and by the following year almost all correspondence was laced with alarm. One girl confided to her South Carolina
kin in 1862, "Oh! Alice, you cannot be thankful enough that your
brothers are not old enough to be soldiers; to be so far away from all that
they are near and dear and we know not what time the sad tidings may
reach us that they are among those who have fallen among the gallant
slain. . . . Oh! Alice since I saw you, so very many of my friends have
been killed. It makes me sad to think of the past." Another Virginia girl
confided, "Let us not be discouraged by these reverses for I feel that
God intends us to separate, or why this entire difference of opinion?"

Why indeed? Many women were stricken with fears and found
few answers to comfort them. And men, whose role it was to reassure,

were caught up in their own anxieties as they watched their hopes for quick victory fade and their dreams of peaceful independence shatter. Within months of secession, nostalgia for the peaceful past prevailed. Mathella Page, the pregnant wife of a soldier, scribbled in January 1862: "We went to Clay Hill to spend the day. Carried the children. I love to go there, they are so kind and affectionate, it recalls the past, too, the voices I used to love, the forms that cheered." Five months later, in May, she was reduced to bearing her child among strangers, a refugee unable to plan for her newborn's future.

Some vainly searched for the silver lining in these gathering clouds. Many, like plantation mistress Kate Stone, celebrated their ethic of independence. She heralded this new era: "Fashion is an obsolete word and just to be decently clad is all we expect. The change in dress, habits and customs is nowhere more striking than in the towns. A year ago even a gentleman never thought of carrying a bundle, even a small one, through the streets. Broadcloth was *de rigueur.* Ceremony and fashion ruled in the land. Presto—change. Now the highest in rank may be seen doing any kind of work that their hands find to do." Stone went on to confide, disingenuously, "In proportion as we have been a race of haughty, indolent, and waited-on people, so now are we ready to do away with all forms of work and wait on ourselves."

ॐ

The patriotic rhetoric mouthed by Southern white women would have caused jeers in the slave quarters. The great majority of African Americans did not support the Confederate war effort. Certainly a small number threw in their lots with Southern whites—although when the free blacks of the Native Guards of New Orleans volunteered for service, they were rejected by Confederate officers. There is little to suggest that the Native Guard was in sympathy with the new government; perhaps they wished to advance equality by loyal service, just in case slave owners triumphed in the rebellion.

Despite the dread of an invading army, many slaves cautiously welcomed the Union soldiers who might prove liberators. Indeed, masters weren't the only ones to go marching off when the war came. Even before Congress passed the 1862 Confiscation Act (repealing the 1792 law that barred blacks from military service) slaves fled plantations, especially in the border states, seeking refuge behind federal lines. A Union officer reported the dangers such escapes entailed: "One negro

IN A SCENE FROM *BIRTH OF A NATION* (1915), A GIRL DECORATES HER DRESS WITH COTTON BOLLS — "SOUTHERN ERMINE" — TO DEMONSTRATE WHITE WOMEN'S SACRIFICE IN THE FACE OF DEFEAT.

man in particular stated to me that he had concealed himself in a swamp for over ten days, watching for an opportunity to escape to our lines, but was detected, put in the stocks and severely whipped." Union officers had diverse responses to these "contrabands," as the escaped slaves were called, some returning them to their owners, still others employing them as teamsters, cooks, and in other service occupations of use to Union operations.

Unofficially, black military units were organized in Kansas, South Carolina, and Louisiana from the earliest days of the conflict. But the flood of black soldiers began in earnest only with the Emancipation Proclamation in January 1863. Later that year more than twenty thousand black volunteers were drawn from the Mississippi Valley alone during the period from Easter to Christmas. Many African-American women joined their husbands behind enemy lines, offering their services as cooks and laundresses to advance the Union cause.

Nearly 200,000 blacks served under the Union flag during the course of the war—almost all enlisted men. Although African Americans made up less than 1 percent of the Northern population, they comprised almost 10 percent of the Union army. Despite Confederate

Refugees along the route of Sherman's March. Both blacks and whites were dislocated by this enormous campaign, which forced evacuation by seizing food supplies and burning out shelters.

Union soldiers and "contrabands," or runaway slaves, work behind federal lines in 1862 to rebuild Culpeper, Virginia.

efforts to stem the flow, the Union drained plantations of slaves. Almost ninety thousand black men from Confederate states donned blue uniforms as approximately 15 percent of the black males in the South between the ages of eighteen and forty-five abandoned their masters, risking all for freedom.

Although most black women were relegated to supporting roles, one of the most intrepid African Americans during the war was Harriet Tubman. Born a slave in Maryland around 1821, she escaped before joining up with abolitionists in Philadelphia. Tubman led several dozen runaways to freedom and became well known as a "conductor" on the Underground Railroad. Before the war broke out she had settled in Canada, but Tubman relocated to Fort Monroe, Virginia, at the start of the conflict. Her services were then requested in occupied South Carolina, where, stationed in Beaufort, she provided Major General David Hunter with invaluable intelligence. Her services as a spy and a scout were critical to Union operations. Tubman dictated a letter back to friends in Boston to entreat their assistance: "In our late expedition up the Combahee river, in coming on board the boat, I was carrying *two pigs* for a sick woman, who had a child to carry, and the order 'double quick' was given, and I started to run, stepped on my dress, it being rather long, and fell and tore it almost off, so that when I got on board the boat there was hardly anything left of it but shreds. I made up my mind then, I would never wear a long dress on another expedition of the kind, but would have a *bloomer* as soon as I could get it. So please make this known to the ladies, if you will, for I expect to have use for it very soon, probably before they can get it to me."

Colonel James Montgomery also employed Tubman's talents, using her to stir slaves into rebellion on Tidewater plantations in the summer of 1863. Within a few months they were able to assist more than 750 low-country slaves to escape rebel masters, severely undermining Confederate morale. Indeed, these exploits were a tremendous boost to the Union. As Tubman explained, "Of these seven hundred and fifty-six, nearly or quite all the able-bodied men have joined the colored regiments here." Tubman conducted these operations with a steep price on her head and with considerable disregard for her own safety. After she helped rescue the slaves, her labors continued: "Among other duties which I have is that of looking after the hospital here for contrabands. Most of those coming from the mainland are very destitute, almost naked. I am trying to find places for those able to work, and provide for them as best I can, so as to lighten the burden on the Government as

HARRIET TUBMAN, SPY AND SCOUT FOR THE UNION, HELPED YANKEE COMMANDERS LEAD HUNDREDS OF SLAVES TO FREEDOM IN THE SOUTH CAROLINA LOW COUNTRY.

much as possible." Despite Tubman's extraordinary exploits and years of service, she was ill rewarded for her patriotism. Paid less than three hundred dollars in all, she died impoverished and in obscurity, denied a pension despite repeated appeals by whites on her behalf.

Tubman was certainly no braver than many of the black men who donned a blue uniform and were threatened with execution if they were captured by Confederate troops. The Confederacy failed to honor the international rules of combat where former slaves were concerned, and even threatened to shoot white officers who commanded black troops.

Army service was an enormous sacrifice for the black enlisted man, with discriminatory pay, degraded treatment, and disproportionate death rates as well. Whereas one in twelve white soldiers in the Union Army died of disease during the war, one in five African-American soldiers did. Combat deaths were equally gruesome. In June 1863 at the battle of Milliken's Bend in Louisiana, one black regiment lost almost half its men.

Despite the inequalities, Union army camps gave many black women and children a refuge from plantation life. To evade the lash of slavery and to flee deteriorating plantation conditions, many slaves abandoned homes to seek a better life—or at least a life that offered hope of freedom. Many knew not what fates might await them, but fervently desired to escape the clutches of the Confederacy. Former slave Mary Barbour recalled her family's flight: "We snook out of de house an' long de woods path, pappy totin' one of de twins an' holding me by de han' an mammy carrying de odder two." After they hooked up with federal troops, her father supported the family by making boots for the army.

Some escaped slaves suffered harassment from former owners. One white Southern woman her former slave reported "begged an' cried," claiming, "'General, dese han's never was in dough—I never made a cake bread in my life; please let me have my cook.'" General Grant refused to intercede, pointing out that the cook was free to leave but "she can do as she likes about it."

Slave women, like their free white counterparts, were thrown into chaos by male relatives' war service. Indeed, such "Confederate treason,"

THIS ILLUSTRATION OF A COOK REFLECTS THE POPULAR, STEREOTYPICAL IMAGE OF BLACK WOMEN IN MEEK, DOMESTIC ROLES.

as siding with the Union was viewed, provoked repercussions. One wife left behind in Missouri confided: "They are treating me worse and worse every day. Our child cries for you. Send me some money as soon as you can for me and my child are almost naked." In Louisiana one Union commander of a black regiment complained: "A practice had largely obtained among owners of female slaves to secure for them free men as husbands—some of these husbands are in my reg't. When it appeared that they had entered the service, they were forbidden by the owners of their wives the permission and privileges

THIS 19TH-CENTURY PAINTING, *MULATTO WOMAN*, IS A SYMPATHETIC AND COMPELLING PORTRAIT OF A NEW ORLEANS WOMAN OF COLOR.

FORMER SLAVE QUARTERS.

before accorded them, and such treatment is practiced upon their wives and children as to exasperate them as has in some instances tended to breaches of the peace."

Many African-American soldiers were driven to desperation by such circumstances. Spottswood Rice wrote to his daughters left behind in rural Missouri: "My respects is worn out and have no sympathy for Slaveholders. And as for her christiantty [the mistress] I expect the Devil has such in hell. You tell her from me that she is the frist christian that I ever hard say that a man could Steal his own child especially out of human bondage." His bravado stemmed from the fact that even as he lay in a hospital bed in Saint Louis, he planned their rescue. "Be assured that I will have you if it cost me my life on the 28th of the mounth," he continued, "8 hundred White and 8 hundred blacke soldiers expects to start up the rivore to Glasgow. . . . when they Come I

A Union solider photographed within the liberated cells at a slave trading company, Price, Birch & Company, in Alexandria, Virginia.

expect to be with them and expect to get you both in return. Dont be uneasy my children."

Desperate circumstances caused drastic results. One Kentucky slave woman spirited her children away, only to be accosted by her master's son-in-law, "who told me that if I did not go back with him he would shoot me. He drew a pistol on me as he made this threat. I could offer no resistance as he constantly kept the pistol pointed at me." She was forced to return home at gunpoint, and the son-in-law kept her seven-year-old as a hostage.

Slave women were not always able to demonstrate opposition with open rebellion. Many expressed resistance to white authority by being recalcitrant concerning plantation duties. For many plantations the enemies within came to represent as much of a threat as fear of invading foes. And the distrust and hardship increased as the war wore on.

The threat of black resistance had created only the faintest frisson of fear in Confederate hearts when white men marched off to war in

AN AFRICAN-AMERICAN WOMAN POSES OUTSIDE THE ABANDONED
PRICE, BIRCH & COMPANY SLAVE TRADING OFFICES.

the spring of 1861. Only in September of the next year, after Lee's advance was stemmed at Antietam Creek, Maryland, and Lincoln issued
a preliminary edict promising to free all slaves in the rebel states, did
the damp chill of doubt creep across the South. But by then most plantation owners were fully mobilized for a prolonged siege, and indeed
the white South, with little dissent, embraced the rebellion. Without
the widespread support of yeoman and merchant classes, the Confederacy would have quickly fallen flat. But female volunteerism was even
more important in launching Confederate independence. Men would
determine the outcome on the field of honor, but women's moral and
material sustenance would enable them to fight.

Arrest of a female Spy

CHAPTER 3

Those Who Served

Those Who
Served

"W hat the event will be of the present secession movements of the South, the Future can only unveil," Jane Pickett wrote to her sister from Yazoo County, Mississippi, in February 1861. Little did she imagine that her husband's prediction "of a *bloody civil war in less than 60 days*" would prove to be deadly accurate. When that war erupted, white women, especially those plantation mistresses whose lives were so invested in slaveowning, were elevated even above the pedestals on which antebellum ideologues had placed them. Fireeaters now expected belles and matrons to play the role of avenging angels, demanding satisfaction, heaping scorn on the Union, and rallying to the Southern cause. The emergence of Confederate nationalism offered Southern ladies unprecedented opportunities to serve.

A mythology about female contributions blossomed in both North and South: stoic mothers, patriotic fiancées, loyal sisters and wives. While the mobilization of forces hit hard throughout the country, Southern women in rural agricultural areas were especially burdened by the departure of so many young white males into the army. Single women and mothers left behind with children found their new positions especially perplexing. Hundreds upon thousands found themselves caught in war's worrying skein. Even those who wished to remain neutral were consumed by wartime inconveniences—the blockade, the shortages, the long lines for every purchase.

All Southern white women were expected to shift their interest and

---

Pages 76–77: A northern sketch portraying the arrest of a Confederate spy.
Opposite: Woman in a Confederate hat.

productive labors from the family circle to the wider Confederate community, to serve the Southern cause. After the bombardment of Fort Sumter, South Carolina, in April 1861 and the Confederate victory at Manassas (Bull Run) three months later in Virginia, women responded to the war machine's voracious demands. But female volunteerism in the North, the Sanitary Commission, Dorothea Dix's nursing corps, Clara Barton's vigilant campaigns, and other Yankee organizational and institutional efforts, far outstripped those of their Southern counterparts.

While women's voluntary movements in the North—from temperance to purity crusades, from missionary work to abolitionist agitation—had flourished for half a century, the Southern social climate was hostile to such activities for women. Even evangelical revivalism had been discouraged in the antebellum era by most slaveholders, who feared such organizing might lead to antislavery crusades, which had been nurtured in the North by women's religious zeal. Virginia Governor David Campbell directed his wife not to attend a Methodist camp meeting in his absence, warning: "Have you not often seen my anxiety about you at those places, and why would you be willing to go to them and run the hazard of being jostled about in a crowd of fanatics without my protecting arm?—Indeed, why go there at all?" Southern ideologues championed mythic visions of women's domesticity—matrons confined completely to the domestic sphere, perched hearthside, tending obedient children and supervising submissive slaves, anxiously anticipating the return of their beloved husbands. This imprisonment was rarely realized in an idyllic form, and its dictates considerably constrained women's choices.

When war finally came, the more autonomous, more independent Yankee women had networks in place and role models to follow for their mobilization. For example on April 19, 1861, more than three thousand women attended a rally staged at New York's Cooper Union. Out of this massive response, the New York Central Association of Relief was founded: twelve of its twenty-five board members were women. This grassroots campaign led to the formation of the U.S. Sanitary Commission, one of the most exemplary mobilizations of civilian labor for war. Southern-born novelist E.D.E.N. Southworth, one of the most successful women writers of her day, had commented in 1855 that "sewing circles and other useful Yankee inventions" were unknown in the South. Such handicaps hampered Confederate campaigns.

While Southern women were at a disadvantage when it came to collective action, many were well-equipped to wage independent strug-

SOUTHERN BELLES OF NORTH CAROLINA.

gles. Plantation mistresses were well schooled in handling their own affairs by planter absenteeism. Women had long been expected to serve as the master's eyes, ears, and perhaps even his voice during prolonged absences. This crucial responsibility—to keep the home fires burning—took on a more urgent cast as the Confederacy coalesced. Southern white women were forced to move outside their own estates to join with neighbors to support the rebellion. The majority restricted themselves to those occupations approved by males, steering clear of controversy during wartime turbulence. Despite the best efforts of these ladies to live up to exalted standards of chivalry, many sacrificed ideals as the war wore on. For women, it was a bumpy road to Confederate heroism.

Females could fulfill their "natural" duties and serve the Confederacy by sewing uniforms, knitting socks, rolling bandages, and performing other volunteer work organized by church groups and local charities in the war's early days. Volunteers were able to complete these tasks in the privacy of their own homes, although some sponsored group events to bring women together for war work and camaraderie. Gaiety pervaded the atmosphere during the war's first months, but by 1862 supplies had become a critical issue within the blockaded South. Women addressed the crisis with ingenuity and vigor, but diminishing festivity, as casualties mounted. Supplying the army with clothing and

WOMEN TREASURED BUTTONS, WHICH GREW MORE AND MORE SCARCE AS THE
WAR WORE ON. MANY WORE THE BUTTONS OF LOVED ONES STRUNG TOGETHER AS
KEEPSAKES AND MEMENTOS AND AS SUBSTITUTES FOR GEMS, WHICH MIGHT
HAVE BEEN SOLD FOR FOOD.

food was a challenge from which they rarely shrank. Whether they
darned and sewed for their own loved ones or for the "sons of the Confederacy," they saw themselves as warriors as much as women.

While Southern mothers nursed and tended to illness within their
own families, often plantation mistresses also supervised care for the
feeble and infirm among their husband's slaves, holding the keys to the
medicine cabinet and a recipe book full of pharmaceutical lore. Some
mistresses might even aid kin or neighbors in the doctor's absence.
Physical drudgery was usually the work of their attendant slaves, but
mistresses were expected to devote time and energy ministering to the
sick. Nevertheless, a lady, in the course of her rounds, would never
jeopardize her reputation by proximity to strangers or intimacy with
the opposite sex.

Army nursing primarily entailed caring for strangers of the opposite sex, a situation that created an artificial barrier to plantation mistresses' rapid assimilation into wartime hospitals. Despite conflicting
loyalties—to serve patriotically without regard to the consequences, or
to remain a lady—many women overcame their doubts, joining the
campaign to supply and staff hospitals for wounded and dying soldiers.
Most launched wartime careers by nursing family members injured in
battle. Richmond's Judith Brockenbrough McGuire sought work in a
local hospital after nursing her nephew, an injured soldier, back to
health. Alabama mistress Augusta J. Evans established a convalescent
home on the grounds of her plantation near Mobile, where she reported

she had spent many "a sleepless vigil by day and night . . . sitting beside one whose life hung upon a slender thread for many days."

Hospitals were founded by industrious women, many impatient with government bureaucracy. Seeing a need, many sprang into action, among them Mrs. Campbell Bruce and Mrs. George Howe, who opened their facility in September 1861 on the state fairgrounds near Columbia, South Carolina. In July of the following year another hospital was established at the state college in town, where more than twenty-five hundred men were treated during the summer. Louisa McCord, a well-known South Carolina writer, lived across the street and worked in the wards. Colleges were emptied of healthy young men one season, and filled with sick and infirm veterans the next. In Virginia a girl reported to her father that the local academy, Washington College, was deserted and more than seven hundred sick soldiers were stationed nearby. "The ladies in town have been preparing supplies out to them," she wrote, "& several of them will go out next week to assist in nursing."

In Montgomery, Alabama, women formed a Ladies' Hospital Association in the early months of 1862. But later in the year the donated cottages of the Soldiers' Home proved inadequate, and women commandeered a three-story building in the center of town. Sophia Gilmer Bibb, a sixty-year-old widow, took charge. Under her leadership, town women set up a workroom where donated supplies were organized and staff remained on call. In addition to their healing duties, Bibb and her staff supervised burial of more than eight hundred men during the war. Her facility became famous, so much so that when she asked Confederate president Jefferson Davis for medical supplies from military warehouses when her stocks ran low, he wrote back, "The surgeon-general has informed me that the ladies' hospital is the best managed and most comfortable one in the Confederacy, and I will take pleasure in giving you carte blanc for anything that may be necessary."

Bibb sparked controversy when she extended her care to wounded prisoners of war, arguing, "They were suffering men and shall be made as comfortable as our Confederate soldiers." But her policy was adopted by many women throughout the South who found themselves holding the hands of dying enemy soldiers. Kate Kern of Winchester, Tennessee, wrote to a Yankee mother: "I sent you a letter the other day informing you of the sad death of your son—Mr. C. J. Presnell; but having to send it by 'Flag of Truce,' I am not sure you will ever receive it." She

LINE DRAWING OF CHARLESTON MANSION FROM EDWARD KING'S
SKETCHES OF THE SOUTH (1873–74).

enclosed a lock of his hair, and promised to track down the particulars of his death and burial. Later Kern wrote back to the mother to report his nurse's account: "On the evening of his death I tried to supply his wants. He could take little nourishment—he asked for ice and wine. This he had and kind attention from the nurses. . . . He gave me no messages. Tho I feel confident he knew he was dying, and did not fear death. In answer to my asking if his Savior was with him, he replied, 'yes—yes'! He died during the night, and was buried the next day in a large double white blanket, as coffins were not then furnished." Kern closed her letter, "Write to me if you can. And love me, for I am your sympathising friend." Certainly the bonds of womanhood could and did, upon occasion, transcend battle lines.

This kind of fraternization with the enemy and familiarity with soldiers still prevented many upper-class women from involving themselves in hospital duties. And so, wealthy and well-born women who entered this service had a great impact as role models. Ella King Newsom, widow of an Arkansas planter, provided an example as valuable as her talents. Trained as a nurse at Memphis City Hospital in December 1861, she traveled in the field with General Albert Sidney Johnston's troops in Kentucky and recruited other women to work with her. She was promoted to superintendent of hospitals in Bowling Green, Kentucky, and served there until the Confederate retreat. Newsom went next to Nashville, then Chattanooga, and finally Atlanta, donating her considerable fortune toward the care of soldiers.

When Cornelia Kincaid wrote to a friend from rural Georgia in 1863 about her mother's plans to become a matron in a hospital in Rome, Georgia, she felt obliged to explain that "some of her acquaintances from Rome, very nice ladies, have gone in as matrons." Many women countered the lingering stigma associated with this work by taking their African-American bondsmen and bondswomen into hospitals and onto the battlefields as a badge of status. We have no record of the slaves' responses to being drafted for such purposes.

Perhaps the most famous Confederate nurse of all, Sally Tompkins, worked side by side with her slaves. Born into a family of wealth and privilege, Tompkins was reared on her family's Virginia plantation, Poplar Grove. Twenty-eight and unmarried when the war broke out, she championed the cause of the Confederate wounded. In Richmond following the first major battle of the war, Bull Run (Manassas), Tompkins wrote to her sister: "It is now nearly 2 o'clock Sunday night—but I am so excited by the news of our glorious victory that I cannot sleep. You have heard by this time of the battle at Manassa on thursday & the enemy had two to one of ours." Moved by the spirit of patriotism, Tompkins persuaded Judge John Robertson to donate his Richmond home to the cause so she could open a hospital. Tompkins ran the Robertson Hospital, which housed more than twelve hundred sick and wounded over its four years of operation before it closed in July 1865. During the war, when President Davis gave Tompkins a military commission as a captain, she accepted her rank but refused a salary. In the postbellum era she became a revered figure.

Tompkins employed both black and white, slave and free, to staff her facility, and other Confederate wards followed suit. Four black matrons and two black women nurses were on staff at General Hospital #10 in Richmond, along with nineteen male slaves and six free black men. By 1863 many free blacks trapped behind Confederate lines and runaway slaves flocked to hospitals for food in exchange for work. The racism imbedded within Confederate society did not always bode well for the African Americans staffing hospitals. Their labor might be welcomed, but white matrons never granted them equal status, and some complained bitterly about blacks' behavior. Indeed, both Phoebe Pember and Kate Cumming, who wrote memoirs about their nursing

SALLY TOMPKINS, REVERED HEROINE OF THE CONFEDERACY, THE ONLY WOMAN GIVEN
A MILITARY RANK, OF CAPTAIN, BY JEFFERSON DAVIS.

experiences, accused blacks of stealing from storerooms, complaints
that echoed the laments of plantation mistresses about their slaves.
Whiskey and other liquor needed for medicinal purposes was in short
supply, kept under lock and key. Supervisors claimed that both drunkenness and "disloyalty" plagued hospitals forced to employ African
Americans. Of course the "loyalty" of slaves and free blacks trapped
within the Confederacy was, quite naturally, a suspect commodity.
Many blacks forced into menial hospital labors responded with pilfer-
ing and belligerence.

A STEREOSCOPIC VIEW OF RICHMOND CITY HOSPITAL.

The routine of the hospital matron was not much different from the endless rounds of the plantation mistress. Nurses provided soldiers with food and drink, wiping their brows and listening to stories of home. Many women wrote and read letters for injured men, and even engineered family reunions. For some nurses the patient's visitors and families could prove challenging. One nurse reported that she had to warn the ladies who frequented the wards to watch their hoop skirts, which might bang into injured limbs dangling off makeshift beds.

Phoebe Pember, a former Charleston belle who was a socially prominent Jewish widow when the war broke out, found her duties as superintendent of the Chimborazo Hospital in Richmond daunting. Pember complained that one of the most persistent problems was the rats: "Other vermin, the change of seasons would rid us of, but the coldest day in winter, and the hottest in summer, made no apparent difference in their vivacious strategy. . . . [They] ate all the poultices applied during the night to the sick, and dragged away the pads stuffed with bran from under the arms and legs of the wounded."

Human problems were even more delicate than pesky rodents. Pember reported that the wife of one of her patients overstayed her welcome and even gave birth to a daughter on her husband's cot. Pember charitably tended to the newborn, who was named Phoebe by the grateful parents. Finally she bought the mother and child rail passage back to rural Virginia, but was dragged into the family drama once again when the infant was abandoned at the railway station. Pember forced her patient out of bed to retrieve his child and was soon able to discharge them both.

Fannie Beers also found herself juggling the complex demands of nursing. Living in Richmond to be near her husband, who served with a Virginia regiment, she was volunteering at the Soldiers' Rest Hospital when she was drafted to organize a medical facility in a warehouse where a gaggle of half-dead Alabama troops had been deposited. Beers rose to the challenge in a matter of hours, creating a hospital to save the dying men. Beers recalled her baptism by fire at the Third Alabama Hospital that first evening: "Four of our sick died that night. I had never in my life witnessed a death-scene before, and had to fight hard to keep down the emotion which would have greatly impaired my usefulness." Beers moved her young son in with her to sleep in the offices provided for her at the warehouse, and devoted herself fully to the newly founded hospital until her husband was transferred. She continued to serve as a matron in four different hospitals in a pattern of travel and service that must have been draining.

Women in the wards found ministering to the suffering and dying to be traumatic and shocking. Kate Cumming of Mobile described a typical scene in April 1862: "The men are lying all over the house on their blankets, just as they were brought from the battlefield. They are in the hall, on the gallery, and crowded into very small rooms. The foul air from this mass of human beings at first made me giddy and sick, but I soon got over it. We have to walk and, when we give the men anything, kneel in blood and water." When Sarah Rice Pryor volunteered to nurse in Richmond after the Seven Days battles (June 25–July 1 1862), she embarrassed herself at first. "As I passed by the rows of occupied cots, I saw a nurse kneeling beside one of them holding a pan for a surgeon. The red stump of an amputated arm was held over it. The next thing I knew I was myself lying on a cot, and a spray of cold water was falling over my face. I had fainted." After a night's rest, Pryor fortified herself with a handkerchief dipped in camphor and returned to the scene of her disgrace. She served twelve-hour shifts (from seven in the morning until seven at night), and was on call in the evenings, a grueling schedule she maintained for over a month.

Some women who at first found their work horrifying became immune to its terrors. Jennie D. Harrold recalled a scene at Seabrook's Warehouse Hospital in Richmond when two black workers came to remove the dying men she was fanning. One of the soldiers complained, "Can't you wait until we are dead?" But she allowed him to be removed without protest, to make room for the wounded pouring in. Selina Johnson, who ministered to the wounded following the second battle of Bull Run (August 29–30, 1862), remembered one patient in particular. "The last few days he lived, the only way he could get any relief from terrible pain was for someone to clasp around the leg with both hands as near where it was cut off as they could and while clasping it tight, press the flesh down over the end of the bone," she wrote. "It was very hard work, so we nurses took turns."

Juliet Hopkins, the wife of the chief justice of Alabama, performed such feats that she was nicknamed "the angel of the Confederacy." During the battle at Seven Pines, Virginia (May 31, 1862), she even went onto the battlefield to tend injured soldiers. She was wounded in the leg while nursing them and spent the rest of her life with a limp due to this injury.

While scores of previously sheltered women confronted the agony of war as they witnessed the lifeblood of thousands ebbing away in hospitals, life-threatening heroics, such as Hopkins's, were not expected of the women of the Confederacy. Celebrated, although rare, were those women who stepped outside the bounds of propriety to endanger their own lives. Hundreds may have witnessed death, but far fewer risked their own in service to the Confederate cause.

∽

Spies were a colorful and exotic breed during the Civil War, and saboteurs and informants were crucial to Confederate victory, especially in the early months of the war. Many white women participated in the effort to betray Union secrets and secure a military advantage. Images of feminine treachery, espionage, and secrecy provided a tangle of violent emotions in the early days of disunion. Although women generally subjected themselves to less danger than men did on behalf of the Confederate

ABOVE: KATE CUMMING, CONFEDERATE NURSE AND DIARIST.

cause—none was hung for her efforts—they nevertheless risked their reputations, and many suffered from the slanders and libels federal authorities heaped on Confederate women spies.

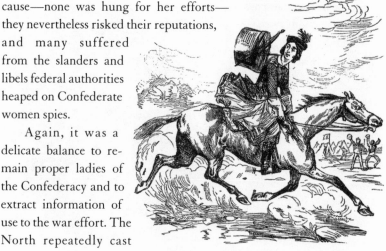

Again, it was a delicate balance to remain proper ladies of the Confederacy and to extract information of use to the war effort. The North repeatedly cast aspersions on the sexual purity of women who gathered intelligence for the Confederacy, branding them as loose women, "Jezebels," and "secesh harlots." It was with this intent that Union General Benjamin Butler issued his infamous Order No. 28 (May 15, 1862), which threatened to treat any New Orleans woman found to be disrespectful of Union soldiers like a "woman of the town plying her trade." The Yankee press also attempted to intimidate Southern women who dared to step outside their appointed sphere of political inactivity. Nonetheless a handful of women were willing to abandon gender dictates, and some managed to obtain a certain fame.

Saboteurs were particularly useful, for they could commit acts that incapacitated and astonished the enemy. Kate Beattie, an energetic Confederate agent, burned Union boats and warehouses, but was neither confined nor executed. Emmeline Piggot, a smuggler and spy working out of New Bern, North Carolina, swallowed evidence of her crime when captured, and although she was convicted of blockade running, she escaped imprisonment. Sarah Jane Smith, captured by Union forces in Missouri in 1864 at the age of sixteen, confessed to a two-year spree of sabotage on the war's southwestern frontier, including destroying four miles of telegraph wires. After conviction of her capital crime, she was sentenced to imprisonment for the duration of the war.

Women smugglers were much more common than women spies, although there is evidence that these activities went hand in hand. The

ABOVE: AN UNFLATTERING CARICATURE OF A CONFEDERATE WOMAN SPY FROM A NORTHERN PERIODICAL.

Those Who Served

extent of women's contribution in these spheres is difficult to document. Although a small circle of female agents has left behind narratives of their adventures, it is far more difficult to reconstruct the careers of scouts and smugglers. But one such unsung heroine, Belle Edmondson, left letters and diaries that offer fragmentary evidence of this type of dramatic undertaking.

The year before the war broke out, Edmondson's family moved from Holly Springs, Mississippi, to nearby Shelby County, Tennessee. Single, twenty-three, and anxious for intrigue, the adventurous young woman was recruited as a scout in 1863 by Confederate officers. Working in and around Memphis, she and some of the other women who assisted the military gradually seem to have forgotten the reticent ways of fine Southern ladies. As one Confederate officer complained, "Some of our best and most polished girls have been gradually driven from the high ground of modest demeanor." Edmondson's wild career may have jeopardized her romance with a Confederate surgeon who broke off his engagement with her during this time. But she was a favorite of the soldiers she helped, who appreciated her daring.

In spite of the constraints imposed by her sex and status, Edmondson was able to contribute greatly to the cause. She described one of her work days in a letter on March 16, 1864: "I began to fix my articles for smuggling, we made a balmorel [petticoat] of Gray cloth for uniform, pin'd the Hats to the inside of my hoops—tied the boots with a strong list, letting them fall directly in front, the cloth having monopolized the back & the Hats the side. All my buttons, brass buttons, Money &c in my bosom. . . . Started to walk, impossible that, hailed a hack—rather suspicious of it, afraid of small pox. . . . Arrived at Pickets, no trouble at all—although I suffered horibly in anticipation of trouble." Although Edmondson was successful in her missions, a few months later federal authorities in Memphis issued a warrant for her arrest. She was forced to flee to an isolated plantation retreat in Mississippi, where she waited out the war.

Although official records fail to supply us with many clues about women's subversive activities, anecdotal evidence survives. Mary Boykin Chesnut reported that "bustles were suspect" and false hair was "searched for papers" when women passed through enemy lines. South Carolina widow Malvina Gist described herself in her diary as a veritable traveling treasure trove. "I am strangely laden; I feel weighed down," she revealed. "Six gold watches are secreted about my person, and more miscellaneous articles of jewelry than would fill a small jewelry

THESE CARICATURES LAMPOON THE NOTION OF FEMALE SPIES BY PLAYING ON
WOMEN'S SOCIAL AND DOMESTIC ROLES.

shop—pins, rings, bracelets, etc." The *Raleigh Weekly Register* recorded a similar story involving Union pickets: "One lady had seven pairs of gaiters, five pairs of boots, five pairs of morocco slippers, three pairs of dancing slippers of white kid, four pairs of India rubber overshoes, and a pair of the longest legged cavalry boots, with double soles, studded with good spikes, heels tapped with shoes of iron. . . . 'How about these, Madam?' said the officer. . . . 'If you will put them on and wear them on your trip to Richmond you can take them, but they can go with you under no other circumstances.'" The woman retreated, put on the boots, and carried them on her feet to a needy soldier.

Many smugglers were involved in schemes to deliver medicine behind Confederate lines, where troops were desperate for drugs and other medical supplies. A niece of the postmaster general, for instance, was caught trying to leave Washington for Virginia with one hundred ounces of quinine sewn into her skirt. Although imprisoned, she was shortly released, as were most women involved in smuggling humanitarian aid.

Passing information through enemy lines was quite easy in the war's early days because there was so much interconnection between Northern and Southern families and travel was frequent. When the pass system restricted travel, women became well practiced in evading pickets. Especially in Virginia, Confederate commanders found information relayed by young women about troop strength and locations to be essential. Confederate officers John Mosby and Jeb Stuart credited youthful female spies Laura Radcliffe and Antonia Ford as critical to their military successes.

One of the most celebrated Confederate heroines, Rose Greenhow, became part of a notorious spy ring in Washington, D.C. With the outbreak of war, Greenhow and her Southern friends were placed under surveillance by Pinkerton agents. Despite her warm relations with prominent Unionists (she was the aunt of Stephen Douglas's wife), the forty-four-year-old widow was placed under house arrest on August 23, 1861, when it was rightfully suspected that she had passed on vital information concerning Union troops before Bull Run.

Fort Greenhow, as her home became known, housed Greenhow and her eight-year-old daughter, as well as several other Washington women, including Eugenia Phillips, a Jewish society hostess, and Ellie Poole, a correspondent for both the *Richmond Enquirer* and the *Baltimore Exchange*. Federal authorities subjected these women to round-the-clock guards. Greenhow objected strenuously, particularly since Federals also incarcerated shady characters in her home as well as society friends. She was appalled by a Mrs. Onderdunk, a woman "of bad repute and recognized by . . . the guard as such, having been seen . . . in the exercises of her vocation." Ladies did not appreciate being called prostitutes or being forced to keep company with them.

These suspected spies were not allowed newspapers, their mail was censored, and only immediate family was afforded supervised visits. Despite these precautions, the women successfully garnered information and passed it to couriers. As a result, in January 1862 Greenhow and her daughter were taken to cells in the Old Capitol Prison where they were held until May. Upon her release, Greenhow was given a patriotic homecoming in Richmond, and Jefferson Davis praised her for her key role in the Bull Run victory. Greenhow continued her intelligence work and in August 1863 undertook a diplomatic mission, ran the blockade, and sailed to Europe, where she put her youngest daughter in a convent school. As Davis's delegate, she was presented to Napoleon III and Queen Victoria. While in London Greenhow published *My Imprisonment and the First Year of Abolition Rule at Washington* to promote the Rebel cause. On her return voyage she was smuggling both gold and secret documents when federal patrols spotted her ship near the shore off Wilmington, North Carolina. Greenhow and two other agents disembarked to a rowboat and tried to reach land and

FROM THE ORIGINAL NEGATIVE   BY BRADY
IN THE COLLECTION OF LC HANDY
WASHINGTON, DC

ROSE GREENHOW, ESPIONAGE AGENT AND MARTYR TO THE CONFEDERATE CAUSE.
SHE AND HER DAUGHTER WERE IMPRISONED BY THE UNION GOVERNMENT AT
THE OLD CAPITOL PRISON.

avoid capture, but their vessel capsized and the trio drowned. Hundreds came to mourn Greenhow at her funeral, and she became a Confederate martyr, a woman who gave her life for her country.

Greenhow's comrade during their Washington imprisonment, Eugenia Phillips, was the wife of a former Alabama congressman. She had been confined for refusing to curb her tongue, but being locked up only increased her resistance to authorities who sanctioned the

OPPOSITE: BELLE BOYD, INTREPID SPY, ELUDED CAPTIVITY AND ESCAPED TO CANADA
AND ON TO ENGLAND DURING THE WAR. HER EXPLOITS BECAME A CONFEDERATE LEGEND.

"imprisonment of women for political opinions." Her incarceration converted her to treason, and when offered the chance to return to Richmond she smuggled important papers to President Davis. Afterward Phillips joined her husband in New Orleans, where the infamous Union general Ben Butler was on the lookout for the equally notorious Mrs. Phillips. Butler accused her of disrespect of the dead when laughter was reported coming from her parlor as a Union funeral contingent passed by her house. On trumped-up charges she was banished to Ship Island, off the Mississippi coast, and held against her will before being deported with her family to a refugee camp in Florida.

The most dashing of women spies within the Confederacy was the young Virginian Belle Boyd. While ostensibly nursing the wounded, she eavesdropped on federal troops and daringly passed her information on to General Stonewall Jackson, among others. When staying in an uncle's Fort Royal, Virginia, hotel she reportedly rode thirty miles in one night to inform on a Union general's plans—then returned before daylight so as not to be discovered gone. In July 1862 she was betrayed, arrested, and imprisoned for a month in the Old Capitol Prison (missing Greenhow by several weeks). Her case provided sensation in the Northern press, with the *New York Herald* painting her a "village courtesan" and a rival paper dubbing her "The Secesh Cleopatra."

Boyd returned behind Confederate lines, but was arrested again and confined to prison. During her second incarceration she

contracted typhoid and was again released. Sailing for England with Confederate documents, she was caught midway across the Atlantic, taken into federal custody, and shipped back to America. The plot thickening, the federal naval officer who captured her, Samuel Hardinage, was then smitten with his prisoner, and allowed her to escape when they docked in Boston. She ended up in Canada and then sailed to London, where she waited for Hardinage, who had promised to marry her. He, meanwhile, was dismissed from Union service before he sailed to England to make Boyd his bride. Hardinage returned alone to the United States to clear his name. Unsuccessful, he became ill and returned to Britain, where he died shortly thereafter, leaving his wife with an infant daughter, a reputation as a traitor, and no means of support. At this point, Belle Boyd cashed in on her notoriety, spending her postwar career trying to live off the Confederate legend she had generated. Indeed she was such a popular performer that imposters sprang up, and she was impelled to carry documents with her at all times to prove her identity.

Even with the postwar records, we have little evidence that legions of women took up espionage. Stories of a few others survive, including that of Sarah Hutchings, who was convicted of sending arms to Confederate guerrilla Harry Gilmore and sentenced to a term of two to five years in 1864 in Fitchburg House of Corrections. Lincoln pardoned her after only a few weeks in response to the public outcry surrounding her case. Maryland woman Bessie Perrine was also arrested for aiding Confederates, but since her trial fell in May 1865, after surrender, she escaped punishment entirely when the courts let her case drop.

Only those women who worked for the Union received pensions or rewards at war's end, including two quite famous turncoats. One, Pauline Cushman, was born in New Orleans and reared in the Midwest before seeking a stage career in New York. Her husband, a theatrical manager, went off to war and died in 1862. On tour in Kentucky in 1863, the young widow drank a toast to Jefferson Davis in the footlights, and became a celebrated Confederate heroine for her act. But it was an act indeed, for Cushman had prearranged with federal authorities to serve as a double agent.

After working in Nashville and behind Confederate lines near Columbia, South Carolina, she was caught, tried for treason, and sentenced to hang. Before the sentence could be carried out, she was rescued by Union troops. After the war she would wear the insignia of a Union major, to which she was entitled.

Although she embellished and elaborated on her daring career, Cushman had indeed passed on critical material to federal authorities during her Union service. Less dramatic but equally successful was Elizabeth Van Lew, the eccentric spinster daughter of a wealthy Virginia slaveowner, who worked for the defeat of the rebels in their own capital throughout the war. Van Lew's neighbors viewed her as overly sympathetic to the Yankees, but never dreamed that she had a pipeline to Ulysses S. Grant or that she had planted her former slave Mary Elizabeth Bowser in the Confederate White House, from where the intrepid African American passed on valuable information. Van Lew served the Union well and when Richmond fell, Grant posted guards outside her house to protect her home. During his presidency he rewarded Van Lew's exemplary loyalty by appointing her post-mistress of Richmond.

The social conditions that fueled the sensationalized interest in Confederate women spies may have had more to do with courting conventions than wartime intelligence. The war took a terrible toll on young women's lives, and federal occupation hemmed them in even more. Those Southern girls who mixed too readily with Yankee soldiers—certainly more frequently than secessionist parents deemed suitable—needed a patriotic excuse for their attentions to Northern soldiers, the only young men available for companionship in the occupied South. Battles depleted Southern communities of bachelors, and fraternization with the enemy was sometimes preferable to no company at all. While this contact was branded disloyal, women might imagine a patriotic content to their encounters with these men if they were ostensibly fishing for information. Further, Union commanders, laying blame for their defeats elsewhere during the war's early years, found it convenient to blame Rebel intelligence rather than superior military strategy. Union commanders complained of leaks concerning troop strength, locations, even the Union battle plan (assuming there was one). Those cunning "secesh" belles were ideal scapegoats.

The Union suggestion that Confederate women served as spies could also effectively besmirch their much-vaunted reputations. Confederates worshiped their mothers, wives, and daughters. Yankees who implied that loosening men's tongues might involve "loosening their collars" simultaneously impugned Southern women's reputations and challenged Confederate manhood. This war of words over women spies revealed in rhetoric and print the depth and scope of the feud.

Women spies on both sides of the war risked death, although none suffered the capital punishment that conviction for treason prescribed. Indeed, ironically, the extreme "gallantry" on both sides during the war prevented women involved in espionage from the severe punishment inflicted on men who committed equal or even lesser crimes. While Union general Ben Butler publicly hanged a male citizen of New Orleans who desecrated the Union flag, women might commit the most heinous crimes and escape execution. Of course few military commanders on either side wished to risk popular backlash by putting a woman to death, whatever crime she committed. However there was an elite handful of women within the South who truly confronted death by serving as comrades-in-arms, disguising themselves in male uniforms and marching into battle.

These brave souls must not be confused with the vivandières or with the "daughters of the regiment" who accompanied enlisted male relatives, staying well behind the battlefront. Sarah Taylor went with the First Tennessee and Lucy Ann Cox was adopted by the Thirteenth Virginia. These young female mascots reflected the spirit of Richmond schoolchildren when they sang:

> *I want to be a soldier,*
> *And with the soldier stand,*
> *A knapsack on my shoulder,*
> *A musket in my hand;*
> *And there beside Jeff Davis*
> *So glorious and so brave,*
> *I'll whip the cussed Yankee*
> *And drive him to his grave.*

This kind of innocent bravado was acceptable, but adult women who actually attempted to carry out the song's message were gender traitors, impermissible patriots. Women dressing as men to serve as soldiers betrayed a fundamental tenet of Confederate faith. Information on women soldiers—those who escaped sexual boundaries to fight as men—is scarce and complicated. We can only make educated guesses about the women who were detected, and have no idea of the number and motives of women who enlisted in either the Union or Confederate armies and served without discovery. As might be expected, there are

The Ladies of New Orleans before General Butler's Proclamation.   After General Butler's Proclamation.

UNION GENERAL BEN BUTLER DECLARED THAT ANY WOMAN IN NEW ORLEANS WHO
SHOWED DISRESPECT TO ANY UNION SOLDIER WOULD BE "TREATED LIKE A WOMAN OF
THE STREETS." HIS ORDER REDUCED PUBLIC MISCHIEF, ALTHOUGH THE LADIES OF
NEW ORLEANS PRIVATELY CURSED "BEAST BUTLER."

more reported cases of Northern than Southern white women mas-
querading as men. Furthermore, only one case of a black woman has
been documented. Also, Emma Edmonds, a Yankee spy, briefly imper-
sonated a young black man during her career. Contemporary accounts
suggested that as many as four hundred cases of women enlisting as
men appeared in military records for the Civil War, but that number
remains unverified.

The few Southern women who have turned up in records as
"enlisted men" afford rare clues about their motives. Some women
donned a uniform and accompanied a sweetheart or husband to the
front. A young wife, Amy Clarke, disguised herself to serve with her
husband and continued as a soldier even after he was killed at the
battle of Shiloh (April 6–7, 1862). Clarke was eventually wounded
and captured by Federals, who gave her a dress and sent her back
behind Confederate lines. Malinda Blalock of North Carolina cut her
hair, put on a loose shirt, and pretended to be her husband's brother to
join up with him when he was drafted into the Confederate army. The
Blalocks, far from patriotic, plotted an elaborate charade to defraud
the army and escape military service, but they were eventually un-
masked and ended up as deserters, fighting with Union guerrilla leader
Colonel George Kirk.

Less than two weeks before the end of the war, Mary Wright and
Margaret Henry were captured and imprisoned; they claimed to have

been fighting undetected for the Confederacy for years. Many women found in uniform were assumed to be prostitutes. Mary and Molly Bell, who had served for two years under the names of Tom Parker and Bob Martin, were accused by officers of being "common camp followers and ... the means of demoralizing several hundred men."

Perhaps some, like the heroine in Rita Mae Brown's novel *High Hearts,* followed their men into war but found themselves confronted by a mix of sensations and unforeseen complications. Certainly some adventurous young women may have been drawn into the great drama by the exodus of hundreds from their midst to join what promised to be the greatest adventure of their lifetime. Many were expert horsewomen, full of a spirit and energy that had no outlet on the home front. If some pursued dreams while others tried to hold on to dreams, we can never ascertain.

One fascinating but unverifiable account of the life of a woman in uniform can be found in *The Woman in Battle: A Narrative of the Exploits, Adventures and Travels of Madame Loreta Janeta Velazquez* (1876). Its author claims to be a widow who assumed a male identity as Lieutenant Henry Buford and became an enterprising and successful Confederate officer. Buford raised his own cavalry company, spied for the Confederacy, served in battle, and was twice wounded. Velazquez even alleges to have romanced women in the line of duty, and provides many other colorful and detailed tales in her remarkable memoir. Velazquez explains: "My enjoyment—if I can designate my peculiar emotions by such a word—I can only attribute to my insatiable love for adventure; to the same overmastering desire to do difficult, dangerous and exciting things, and to accomplish hazardous enterprises, that had induced me to assume the dress of the other sex, and to figure as a soldier on the battle-field." When her narrative appeared in 1876, it stirred quite a controversy and provoked Confederate general Jubal Early to denounce the falsehoods and inconsistencies he found in her text. We do have evidence concerning Henry Buford, and some of his exploits are verifiable. However, the "fact" of Velazquez and Buford being one and the same remains unproven, as are many of Velazquez's claims in her memoir. Whether or not her story was true, the account provides one woman's explanation for the sort of masquerade we know some valiant women undertook.

Better documented than the tales of women in uniform are the stories of women in government jobs during the war. By working in the public realm they were assuming a man's role, but in a less threatening, more socially acceptable manner. We do know that "the most high born ladies filled these places as well as the humble poor," and such famous South Carolina names as Rhett, Huger, and Izard are found on the pay-roll of the treasury office in Columbia, South Carolina. What we don't know is how this government service changed women's expectations, what opportunities it offered them, and in what way they experienced these challenges. Our interpretation of their historical saga, again, is limited to a select body of documentation.

Annual salaries for government clerks increased rapidly during the Civil War, from five hundred dollars in 1862 to three thousand dollars in 1864, but not fast enough to keep up with wartime inflation. In addition, the Confederate scrip in which CSA employees were paid became worth increasingly less. However, while women were initially paid half a man's salary, by war's end they were earning equal compensation. We cannot yet determine what contributed to this development: Were pay scales upgraded once women had been trained? Did pay equity arise in response to women's demands? We do know that in December 1863 single women working in a government arms factory struck for higher wages, demanding to be paid the two dollars more per day earned by married women. Although the government responded by advertising for three hundred replacements, the Confederate Congress did establish a committee to investigate complaints as a result of the strike.

Women in government arms factories often had more pressing concerns than pay equity. As a paper in the Confederate capital reported on March 15, 1863, "Richmond was greatly shocked on Friday by the blowing up of the Laboratory, in which women, girls, and boys were employed making cartridges; ten women and girls killed on the spot, and many more will probably die from their wounds." The accident left forty dead and twenty-nine injured. Later in the year in a similar mishap in Jackson, Mississippi, ten women perished.

Working in mills and factories were poor prospects during wartime, and few plantation mistresses were forced into such desperate straits. The plight of mill hands was harsh, but not as risky as employment in an arms factory. The situation wasn't eased by the fact that Union troops targeted both these industries. During his infamous scorched earth campaign, General William Tecumseh Sherman torched a cotton mill in Saluda, South Carolina, and then forced four hundred women from nearby rural Georgia to march ten miles to the nearest railroad depot where they could be deported northward. Contemporary folklore has the despised Union general claiming that the women

FLEEING BEFORE SHERMAN'S GRAND MARCH.

FLEEING BEFORE SHERMAN'S GRAND MARCH DEPICTS ONE OF THE MOST DREADED
CAMPAIGNS OF THE WAR FOR CONFEDERATE CIVILIANS.

were all prostitutes and shipping them out to keep the Rebel harlots
away from his troops. But whether they were common camp followers or
merely women burned out of their factories, they reflected the growing
number of female poor.

The majority of white women on plantations did not become homeless indigents, although there are accounts of women from wealthy
families reduced to seeking any kind of work at all by war's end. Some
impoverished planters turned slaves off the land, unwilling or unable to
continue to feed black dependents when white families faced dwindling
storehouses. Slave women might be thrown off estates, while white
women could be driven from their homes by invading troops. But more
commonly, wives, black and white, anchored themselves in their hus-
bandless homes, trying to hold the household together in terrible times.
Mistress and slave mother might share in this effort to keep children fed
and families protected from plundering troops—but with opposite
goals in mind.

๑

As the war dragged on, it became more problematic for African Americans to define their enemy. Certainly slavery headed the list, and most
slave owners were a close second. But could the Union army be a foe if

it liberated blacks? Most slaves were well aware that they, not the Union, were responsible for emancipating themselves, but the question remained, would either former masters or invading Yankees provide them with opportunities to exercise, extend and protect the liberties newly seized? African-American women who wished to "serve" were offered complex and contradictory choices. Certainly the Confederacy failed to solicit or acknowledge their roles. Many thousands chose to flee plantations, to strike out for Union protection.

The tales of heroic black Southern women are buried deep within the past. We can well imagine that most African-American women patriotically served their own cause—not that of Rebel masters, but the promise of freedom sweeping in from the North. But it is exceptionally difficult for us to know the concrete details of black women's roles during the war, for to date we have only one published Civil War memoir by an African-American woman, who fled from white owners to join the Union army.

Susie King Taylor was born on a Georgia plantation in 1848, the first child of a domestic slave woman named Baker. Her grandmother had been born in 1820, the granddaughter of an African slave brought to Georgia during the 1730s. Taylor lived with her grandmother, a slave in Savannah, leaving the plantation when just a young girl. During her childhood years as a city slave she was fortunate to have white playmates willing to teach her to read and write (offering instruction to a slave was against the law). Ironically, one of her tutors abandoned her to serve with the Savannah Volunteer Guards when the war broke out in 1861. Taylor vividly recalled the shelling of the port, which prompted her return to the country to be with her mother: "I remember what a roar and din the guns made. They jarred the earth for miles." When Federals captured nearby Fort Pulaski, Georgia, Taylor went with an uncle to escape slavery and was ferried behind Union lines to Saint Simons Island, one of the Sea Islands off the Georgia coast. Because she was literate and impressed white officers, she was enlisted at the age of fourteen to teach freed slaves how to read and write. Later she married a sergeant with the First South Carolina Volunteers, a black regiment, and subsequently served alongside her husband as a nurse and laundress for the troops. Taylor practiced other skills as well, and confided, "I learned to handle a musket very well while in the regiment, and could shoot straight and often hit the target." When Clara Barton came to the Sea Islands, Taylor worked alongside her. She remained with her husband's regiment through February 1865.

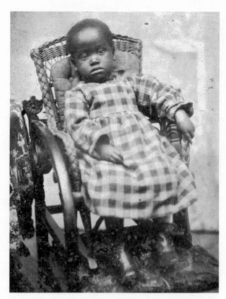

After the war Taylor resettled in Savannah and opened a school. But when her husband died during her pregnancy in 1866, she faced an uncertain and unsettling future, left as she was "soon to welcome a little stranger alone." By 1868 she was forced to close the school, and in 1872 she left her child with her parents and took a job as a domestic for a wealthy Savannah family. Unlike many women of her race and class, she did not spend the rest of her years in this role, slavery's legacy. Rather, she was able to move to Boston, remarry, and embark on a career as a club-woman and civic activist. In 1902 she published *Reminiscences of My Life in Camp with the 33rd United States Colored Troops, Late 1st S.C. Volunteers,* a chronicle of her life told with poignant insight.

Despite the great rarity of her account, Taylor made a point in *Reminiscences* of reminding the world that she was by no means alone:

> There are many people who do not know what some of the colored women did during the war. There were hundreds of them who assisted the Union soldiers by hiding them and helping them to escape. Many were punished for taking food to the prison stockades for the prisoners.... Others assisted in various ways the Union army. These things should be kept in history before the people. There has never been a greater war in the United States than the one of 1861, where so many lives were lost—not men alone but noble women as well.

Taylor testifies that white women were not the only noble women of the South during the prolonged siege of the 1860s. And her rebuke remains an unanswered plea for our appreciation of the heroics of African American women in wartime. Until we more fully integrate

---

ABOVE: PORTRAIT OF AN UNIDENTIFIED SOUTHERN BLACK CHILD, CIRCA 1890.

ABOVE: UNIDENTIFIED LOUISIANA WOMEN OF COLOR, READING. THESE STYLIZED, GENTEEL IMAGES OF AFRICAN-AMERICAN WOMEN ARE RARE. THEY MAINLY DEPICT CREOLES IN NEW ORLEANS, WHO CULTIVATED A SEPARATE AND ELITE MIXED-RACE COMMUNITY.

race and gender into our reconstructions of Southern history, with careful attention to the significant yet neglected role of black women, until we recognize that the Civil War's outcome was influenced by events on the homefront as well as the battlefield, we can never really comprehend the war in its fullest dimensions.

CHAPTER 4

Those Who Also Served: Back on the Land

Those Who Also Served: Back on the Land

Plantations were an integral part of wartime strategy, and the Confederate government made that clear. Without planter cooperation, the war effort was doomed. Agriculture was more necessary than ever to Southern strategy, and planters were urged to grow crops to feed the army, rather than staples like cotton and indigo. A campaign of patriotic coercion followed. "Plant corn and be free, or plant cotton and be whipped." With many states complying dramatically, the South's cotton crop dropped from 4.5 million bales in 1861 to 1.5 million the next year. But as private speculators sought out cotton, many farmers had to be dissuaded from growing the valuable crop. Hoarding and smuggling were tempting. Some planters hoped to make a killing in cotton, like Mississippi planter James Alcorn who continued to grow and trade, despite his wife's pleas that he join her in safety in Alabama where she was a refugee. Many more planters supported the government by abandoning the cash crop in favor of foodstuffs, and their wives had a vital role in this wartime venture.

Most plantation mistresses chose to remain on the land, despite the escape their wealth offered them. This required a great deal of bravery and fortitude, especially during the many planting seasons, droughts, and disappointing harvests that followed; these ordeals, of course, they shared with the wives of yeomen farmers. Additionally, the hardships confronted by plantation women were multiplied by the threat of enemy invasion, the pinch created by both the blockade and

PAGES 106–7: WALKER PLANTATION.
OPPOSITE: THE BOOK IS A SYMBOL OF FREEDOM IN THIS STYLIZED PORTRAIT OF AFRICAN AMERICANS.

governmental requisitions, as well as the growing resistance if not out-right rebellion of the black labor force. Planter women couched their decisions to stay not in terms of patriotism but as pure practicality—someone had to keep the home fires burning. Nonetheless, Confederate statesmen capitalized on this important dimension of homefront loyalty, urging women to remain steadfast and patriotic by toiling in their own fields, while men marched off to battle.

Statesmen and soldier alike initially had few fears for women anchored on the land in relative isolation, in backwoods or upcountry, on large estates or small. Confederate patriots rallied troops with little concern for families left behind. Because the Civil War was a "brothers' war," at the outset few feared the kind of bloodbath and retribution that war often brings to civilians; military leaders expected chivalry to extend well beyond the usual bounds, and confine violence to the battlefields. Few if any could imagine the kind of "total war" to which the Union would resort, most especially by the conflict's final months.

When General William T. Sherman's Union troops were marching from Atlanta to Savannah in the fall of 1864 during what was perhaps the war's most infamous campaign, myth and mishap mixed to shape many legends. One tale about the march predictably exalts the powers of a Southern lady against Yankee invasion. Sherman's troops were ransacking a mansion near Cartersville, Georgia, on the banks of the Etowah River when a slave wailed, "What is Miss Cecilia going to do now?" Allegedly, Sherman overheard and found out that "Miss Cecilia" was a noted belle he had courted at West Point many summers before the war. He ordered the soldiers to replace what they had taken, put a guard on the house, and left a note:

Dear Madam:
You once said that you would pity the man who would ever become my enemy. My answer was that I would ever protect and shield you. That I have done. Forgive me all else. I am but a soldier.
Respectfully, William T. Sherman

This is one of the rare instances among the hundreds of legends surrounding Sherman that paints the Union general as something besides a heartless brute. Sherman in Georgia, Benjamin Butler in Louisiana, and David Hunter in Carolina—along with many other Union comrades—were reviled in the South during wartime and their names spat out as obscenities after surrender.

By the fall of 1863, in the wake of the victory at Gettysburg and after the fall of Vicksburg, the Union resorted to the harshest military tactics to demoralize soldiers and citizens alike: the scorched earth policy, the liberation of slaves and arming them against former masters, and terrorism aimed at civilians. Sherman's notorious "march to the sea" pushed the war to new heights of violence and cranked Rebel vituperation several decibels higher. In December 1863 the Confederate Congress lashed out:

> Accompanied by every act of cruelty and pain, the conduct of the enemy has been destitute of that forbearance and magnanimity which civilization and Christianity have introduced to mitigate the asperities of war. Houses are pillaged and burned, churches are defaced, towns are ransacked, clothing of women and infants is stripped from their persons, jewelry and mementoes of the dead are stolen, mills and implements of agriculture are destroyed, private salt works are broken up, the introduction of medicine is forbidden, means of subsistence are wantonly wasted to produce beggary, prisoners are returned with contagious diseases, the last morsel of food has been taken from families . . . helpless women

CONTRABANDS WITH THE UNION ARMY.

have been exposed to the most cruel outrages and to that dishonor which is infinitely worse than death.

Portraying the Union army as marauding rapists did not effectively counteract federal terrorism, but it perhaps heightened fears for women left behind on plantations. Women, after all, were not expected to fight off invaders but to tend the home fires. One diarist confided: "The real sorrows of war, like those of drunkenness, always fall most heavily upon women. They may not bear arms. They may not even share the triumphs which compensate their brethren for toil and suffering and danger. They must sit still and endure." But this was clearly romanticization; few had the luxury of sitting still.

Confederate women nevertheless harped on this theme of gender duty. As Louisianian Sarah Morgan declared, "To feed, to clothe, to teach, to guide, to comfort, to nurse, to provide for and to watch over a great household, and keep its complex machinery in noiseless order— these were the women's rights which she asserted." But not all Southern women were so enthusiastic. Mary Boykin Chesnut chafed at stereotypical notions of women's duties: "South Carolina as a rule does not think it necessary for women to have any existence outside of their pantries or nurseries. If they have none, let them nurse the bare walls. But for men! the pleasures of all the world are reserved." As a bright, talented, and childless woman, Chesnut was especially hemmed in by patriarchal dictates.

Unfortunately for men, at the time of the Civil War the pleasures of the world were to don uniforms and prepare to die, in camp or in hospital if not while fighting (in fact, two soldiers died from disease for every battle death). These ghastly death scenes were often conveyed in letters home, such as those Virginian Margaret Junkin Preston's husband sent. "Such pictures of horrors as Mr. P gives!" she wrote. "Unnumbered dead Federal soldiers cover the battle field, one hundred in one gully, uncovered and rotting in the sun, they were all strewn along the roadside. And dead horses everywhere by the hundred. Hospitals crowded to excess and loathsome beyond expressions in many instances. How fearful is war! I cannot put down the details he gave me, they are too horrible." Women might not have witnessed these bloodcurdling spectacles, but men's need for comfort hardly spared them.

Mothers, wives, and sisters suffered from melancholy as war worn on. Louisa Henry, anchored to her Mississippi River plantation, Arcadia, wrote to her mother in 1862: "I feel 10 years older than when the war commenced—and look at least five years older. I can see the change myself and my hair is turning grey rapidly." Two years later she had been driven off her plantation and was hiding from Federals in a cottage in the woods. "Ma, sometimes I feel *almost* desperate," she wrote, "and almost wish I could take a Rip Van Winkle sleep till all is over and settled."

These profound transformations were evident throughout the South. Confederate Sarah Dawson commented: "Were these same people—these haggard, wrinkled women, bowed with care and trouble, sorrow and unusual toil? These tame, pale, tearless girls, from whose soft flesh the witching dimples had long since departed or were drawn down into furrow—were they the same school girls of 1861?" Adolescents were sobered by grief, among them eighteen-year-old Amanda Worthington in Mississippi, who stopped writing in her diary for a year after her brother Bert died in the war. When she recommenced, she reflected: "What a change has passed over my life since last I kept a journal! Deep have I drank of the bitter waters of sorrow and the lightness of heart that once was mine will never return me more."

Many women lost not only husbands, but all hope. In February 1863 Mary Vaughn, nearly mad with grief, wrote from her plantation home, ironically named Sunny Side:

I do not think I am so much more sinful than others that he [God] should clutch my heart strings with his iron hand and tear them one by one asunder. First he took my dear greyhaired Father who had always been so dear and indulgent to me, but Charlie was left to me, and well did he fill the place of Father and husband to me. Then little Willie [her infant son], still I did not murmur, but now, oh how, can I lift my voice in praise to Him who has taken from me the one hope of my life. I don't think I have had one thought apart from Charlie since we married. My every wish has been to try in some measure to return his devotion and untiring kindness. I cannot for the life of me realize my forlorn situation. He must come home yet. It cannot be true he has left me to suffer and endure alone. He always would shield me from everything like trouble and annoyance, how can I walk the dark future alone and unassisted by his strong arm of protection. I have but one wish and that is to die. You speak of my baby. Why, sister, will not God smite me there too? Will he not darken my young life to the utter most. I will crush back the love, welling up in the depths of

YOUNG CONFEDERATE GIRL IN VARINALAND, VIRGINIA IN 1864. THIS SETTLEMENT
WAS PRESUMABLY NAMED AFTER THE CONFEDERATE FIRST LADY, VARINA DAVIS.

my heart for the little one, so when God lays his chilling hand
upon her limbs, it will not craze me. I have not read my bible
since Charlie died. My tears and feelings seem frozen. I know,
I feel but one thing, I am alone, utterly desolate.

The near-suicidal widow renamed her baby girl "Charlie," symbolic of
her warring feelings of denial and memorialization.

Even those plantation mistresses who did not lose a family member to
war had friends and neighbors who did. The Confederate losses were so
enormous and devastating that the federal army seemed to be winning
the war through attrition. Even when Confederate troops lost fewer
men than the Union side in a battle, generals in gray almost always lost a
greater percentage of their fighting force. By September 1862 the Confederate Congress was desperate enough to push through a draft law
that raised the upper age of conscription from thirty-five to forty-five.

The government compounded the tension in reference to the draft by instituting the infamous "twenty Negro law" in October 1862, whereby any white man was exempt from army service who could demonstrate a managerial role for twenty slaves or more (both owners and overseers qualified). President Jefferson Davis supported this measure ostensibly to keep the Confederacy fed, but that argument backfired: farm families were outraged that planters, who could easily afford to avoid service by having substitutes, were now further legitimated if they sat out the war. These extremely unpopular measures coincided with failing harvests, sparking sedition and unrest. Within the Confederacy only four thousand to five thousand men were granted government exemptions in nineteen categories ranging from occupational emergency (apothecaries) to physical disability (blindness). Of those exempted, only 3 percent took advantage of the "twenty Negro law," and on 85 percent of these plantations where white men could prove eligibility, no exemption was taken. Nevertheless, the perception of class privilege rankled the populace and created a public relations disaster. Even the five-hundred-dollar tax levied on the exempted, instituted in May 1863, did not mollify critics. Divided ranks could and did weaken Confederate resolve.

Daily life without the company or assistance of men drove women in some areas of the South to desperate measures. In one instance a group of seventeen South Carolina women pleaded with the governor not to draft a man named Erwin Midlen because "he had done all our hawling for the last three years and attended to our domestic Business as we could not Procure any other man to do—see to our hawling and other business as our Husbands are all in the army and some of them killed and some died in service. And we are all poor without any means of doing our hawling we have no horses nor wagons of any kind." Whether the "sickly and feeble man" was spared by this petition is not recorded.

By 1864, when plantation mistress Clara Bowen was joined by her husband for a week's furlough, she wrote to a friend: "Do not call me unpatriotic, Alice! I am sure farmers are as necessary to our suffering country as soldiers. Food and clothing must be made for the army as well as for the women and children—starvation would be a more powerful foe than those we are now contending with." By the time Bowen wrote this letter from Ashtabula, South Carolina, Southern agriculture was already in ruins, with black and white manpower in desperately short supply.

Slave men were also being drafted into government service by the war's second year, perhaps in an effort to keep Confederate guard over valuable African-American labor, which was being spirited away for the Union cause. Blacks were forced to serve as nurses in government hospitals, drivers of supply wagons and ambulances, and cooks within Confederate camps. Most important to the war effort, the war department could and often did have the authority to impress slave labor into service to build earthen fortifications around cities. Louisa McCord Smythe, daughter of South Carolina writer Louisa McCord, recalled that family slaves were donated to the work effort in wartime South Carolina. "Later on when the work of keeping up all those fortifications under fire became tremendous," she recalled, "numbers of negroes were sent over, from the upper districts as well as the low country to help. I remember my Mother going to Lang Syne to start her squad off."

The role black Southerners played during the Civil War remained central, both symbolically and practically. Statesman William Cabell Rives proclaimed at the outset that it was not a question of slavery at all, but a question of race. But racial hegemony was hard to maintain during wartime—indeed by the last few weeks of the war, the Confederate government was willing to consider arming blacks in a desperate bid to continue the losing battle. As early as 1863 with the Emancipation Proclamation, the floodgates of freedom had opened wide to African Americans, who seized the opportunity to escape. For those whites left behind on plantations, the process was painful to witness, for the spirit of emancipation created not so much a tidal wave of resistance to the Confederate cause as a strong and constant flow that washed over the South, eroding slaveholders' power day by day.

The weakening of the Confederacy was most visible in those areas of the occupied South where escaped slaves, called contrabands, settled with their families and expropriated Confederate lands—with the blessings of the federal government, which leased them the property. On the South Carolina Sea Islands a thriving community of ten thousand blacks was established when Federals conquered and secured the region in 1862—a community that historian Willie Lee Rose has called a "rehearsal for Reconstruction." Northern teachers then moved down to help educate the newly freed residents, including Charlotte Forten, a young woman born into a prominent free black family in Philadelphia and educated in Salem, Massachusetts. Forten felt excited by the challenge of traveling South to help the freed people, and settled in at Saint Helena Island as the lone black in the colony of Northern teachers. In

LEAVING CHARLESTON ON THE CITY BEING BOMBARDED.

SKETCH OF MEN, WOMEN, AND CHILDREN FLEEING CHARLESTON DURING
A UNION INVASION.

May 1864 the *Atlantic Monthly* published a two-part article chronicling her experiences called "Life on the Sea Islands," which provides a vivid record of this dramatic episode. She found her pupils diligent: "I wish some of those persons at the North who say the race is hopelessly and naturally inferior could see the readiness with which these children, so long oppressed and deprived of every privilege, learn and understand." And white officers in the region were mesmerized by the transformation African Americans were able to make, seizing fully their opportunity to homestead the land. When this experiment proved successful, federal authorities sold some of the Sea Island property to blacks at auctions for unpaid taxes.

Another successful experiment was conducted at Davis Bend, Mississippi—on land owned by the family of the Confederate president. Davis's brother was forced to abandon his plantation in 1862, but was unable to convince his slaves to accompany him. When Union troops arrived they discovered that blacks had expropriated the big house and were managing the place efficiently. By 1865 these self-sufficient African Americans turned the plantation into what General U. S. Grant called "a negro paradise." The workers cultivated two thousand bales of cotton for a profit of $160,000.

In Louisiana, Union general Nathaniel P. Banks converted fifty thousand former slaves into wage laborers on fifteen hundred plantations owned or managed by the federal government. And in 1865

General William T. Sherman established a "black colony," a thirty-mile-wide coastal strip from Charleston, South Carolina, to the Saint Johns River in Florida: black homesteaders were allowed forty-acre parcels by federal authorities and it was here perhaps that the phrase "forty acres and a mule" was born.

Despite these Union efforts, the majority of enslaved blacks, the majority women and children without resources and in a dangerous, war-torn region, did not escape bondage until after Appomattox. These blacks, anchored unfree on plantations, were restless from the war's earliest days, just waiting to rip away from their moorings. A white widow on her Natchez Trace plantation wrote to her sister in early 1861: "I want to sell and go father north where everything is calm and quiet. . . . Can we cope with an enemy abroad & one at home—negros are fully alive to the state of things & are much more sensible than one would suppose." She confessed to bouts of paranoia. "I can imagine all sorts of noises at night and sometimes think they are right at my door. One night I took a large paper of powder & matches & put them at the door to blow up the whole affair."

Planters felt deep ambivalence about the matter of slave "loyalty," hoping slaves would stand by masters but fearing they would abscond, if not openly rebel. At the same time, many women expressed complex sentiments, among them Mary B. Chesnut, who commented on a slave insurrection: "I have never thought of being afraid of negroes. I had never injured any of them; why should they want to hurt me?" Even after her cousin was strangled by slaves on a nearby plantation, she asserted; "But nobody is afraid of their own negroes. These [her cousin's murderers] are horrid brutes—savages, monsters—but I find everyone, like myself, ready to trust their own yard." Her claim cannot be dismissed as innocent bravado nor as propaganda. Rather, Chesnut, like women of her race and class, repressed fear of slaves, maintaining the pretense that their own enslaved African Americans were happy, childlike creatures.

This pretense was challenged dramatically by rebellious and runaway slaves. In the fall of 1861 in Adams County, Mississippi, planters conducted kangaroo trials of slaves suspected of plotting a conspiracy. In a record of their testimony, slaves did indeed confess to plans of murder and rape; hangings in a nearby orchard followed. Paranoia and precautions continued throughout the war, throughout the Confederacy. In February 1863 Virginian Lucy Johnston Ambler, age sixty-three, confided to her diary, "I intend to get Mr. Downs to show me how to shoot tomorrow and how to load." South Carolinian Melissa Fouche wrote in January 1863 from her home in Ninety-Six, "It has gotten to be very common with the darkies about here when they get the least offended with the owners to give them poison in their victuals. Maj. Griffins house girl put something in their coffee but they detected it before drinking enough to effect."

Rape and murder were extreme cases of slave rebellion, much less likely than the most common form of resistance—running away. Slave desertion of plantations was an integral part of life in wartime, and ironically, as one woman complained, "those we loved best, and who loved us best—as we thought—were the first to leave." Seventeen slaves fled the Wickham plantation in Hanover

County, Virginia, in June 1862 and another seventeen were "carried off" by Union troops between June 26 and July 5, 1863. More than 250 slaves remained behind, but the planter, who listed the name and age of every missing slave in his personal papers, considered this loss a crushing blow. Slaves fleeing behind enemy lines did not represent just a loss of income, but equally a loss of face. A story appeared in the abolitionist newspaper *The Liberator* in August 1862 that recounted a conversation between a mistress and her slave, and the former's humiliation when a Yankee gunboat landed nearby: "'Now, 'member I brought you up. You won't take your children away from me, will you, Mill?' 'Mistress I shall take what children I've got lef'.' 'If they fine that trunk o' money or silver plate you'll say its your'n, won't you?' 'Mistress, I can't lie over that. You bo't that silver plate when you sole my three children.'" The slave is further vindicated when she relates: "Here comes in four sojers with swords hangin' to their sides, an' never looked at mistress, but said to me, 'Auntie, you want to go with us?' 'Yes, sir,' I said. . . . and we all

---

ABOVE: KADY BROWNELL, A UNION WOMAN WHO TRAVELED WITH HER HUSBAND'S RHODE ISLAND REGIMENT. PHOTOGRAPHS OF SOUTHERN WOMEN WHO ACCOMPANIED THE CONFEDERATE ARMY HAVE NOT YET SURFACED.

A CROQUET MATCH DURING WARTIME. THE SOLE AFRICAN-AMERICAN SUBJECT
IN THE SHOT IS NEARLY LOST IN THE LEFT BACKGROUND OF THE PICTURE.

got on the boat in a hurry; an' when we's fairly out in the middle of the
river, we all give three times three cheers."

Why were slave owners determined to depict slavery as such a
pleasant paternalistic system if it was so evidently anathema to blacks?
Confederates again and again portrayed scenes of slave loyalty, including this reported dialogue between a master and slave: "'Do you
want to go to the Yankees? You have my consent, if you do though
I should grieve to part with you old fellow,' his master said affectionately." And followed the formulaic reply: "Laws, no, Mas' John. I
doesn't want to go wid de Yanks'. I never wants to see no mo' Yanks,
'cepting dey's dead ones."

Black voices produced by white ventriloquism qualify as dubious
evidence—both the testimony of white Union soldiers and African
Americans frequently contradict this Confederate lore. In truth slaves
risked life and limb to escape. Confederate scout Belle Edmondson
described rounding up runaways in Shelby County, Tennessee: "A family of negroes had got this far on their journey from Hernando to Memphis when Mr. Brent met them, and they ordered him to surrender to
a Negro, he fired five times, being all the loads he had—killed one

Negro, wounded another, he ran in the woods and we saw nothing more of him—one of the women and a little boy succeeded in getting off also." For the first time since the American Revolution, large numbers of women and children found freedom by deserting behind enemy lines. One mistress complained that slaves "in some cases have left the plantations in a perfect stampede."

Some blacks who went to become Union soldiers left behind families subject to considerable hardship. A Union provost marshal reported in March 1864: "The wife of a colored recruit came into my Office to night and says she has been severely beaten and driven from home by her master and owner. She has a child some two years old with her, and says she left two larger ones at home." Planters and wives left to manage with depleting resources and a recalcitrant labor force took out their frustrations on remaining slaves. Plantation mistress Emma LeConte complained: "The field negroes are in a dreadful state; they will not work, but either roam the country, or sit in their houses. . . . I do not see how we are to live in this country without rule or regulation."

As the war went on the lack of food and material comforts became so severe that some planters, to conserve supplies, simply turned slaves off the land. Virginian Mary Stribling reported that by the time of the Emancipation Proclamation her father had already warned slave women and children that he would sell the "useless" ones who could not earn their own keep. Mistresses, deprived of slaves, were thrown onto their own. The wife of a Confederate soldier, Sallie Brock, confided that she "was forced to go out into the woods nearby and with my two little boys pick up faggots to cook the scanty food left to me."

Adding to the burden of Confederate households in this time of

ABOVE: EMMA LECONTE, A SOUTH CAROLINA BELLE WHO LEFT AN INSIGHTFUL DIARY OF HER WARTIME ADVENTURES.

scarcity was the need—indeed the duty—to contribute to the Confederate cause. As one Mississippi mistress explained: "My heart has yearned over our brave, noble, bare-footed ragged young men, & have done all I could in my limited way to meet their necessities. Our stock of cloth laid up for the negroes is almost exhausted, having given suits of clothes to the soldiers. We also have given hundreds of pairs of socks, the amount of 500 I think to the Army. Some three or four weeks since we sent twelve blankets, eight dozen pairs of socks, three carpet blankets, to Genl. Prices Army." Virginia matron Sallie Moore remembered, "We had even cut up our carpets into lengths and sent them to camps for the soldiers to sleep on."

Besides the endless production of supplies, plantations were expected to host Confederate soldiers. In South Carolina, writer Louisa McCord composed a letter to one of her son's army friends in August 1863: "in case of your being sick or wounded, you will always find a room & a welcome with me. My vocation is to help soldiers, & when the soldier is a friend, I am only the more ready for my duty."

Many gave generously to the anonymous sons of the Confederacy who imposed on their hospitality. After Yankees burned her home, Rebecca Ridley lived in the cookhouse of her former plantation, Fair Mont, outside Murfreesboro, Tennessee. Following a battle she reported: "The ground has been covered with snow and ice—freezing our poor unprotected soldiers—some of them I understand are bare-footed, none have tents—or a sufficiency of blankets and all have to depend on the country for subsistence—poor fellows, how my heart bleeds for them. They come in at the houses to get warm, and get something to eat, and some of our citizens who pretend to be very Southern grudge them the food they eat—say they will be eat out." Patriot Katie Miller reported to her aunt, "I told ma when *provisions* got so low that she couldn't feed a passing soldier to let me know everytime one comes and I would go minus one meal for him."

Slaves running off to "Lincoln land" and bare pantries were sacrifices mistresses shouldered with dignity, but the burdens of contact with Yankees, which increased as incursions and defeats mounted, were unbearable to most Southern white women. A Charleston newspaper reported the "suffering" of Confederate women as they were searched at Yankee pickets near Norfolk:

> The creature selected for this business is a villainous, hagish looking old woman, who glories in being the widow of the notorious

John Brown who met so just a fate at the gallows at Charlestown, Va. Ladies are required to divest themselves of all clothing save their chemisettes and even their shoes are not unfrequently taken off and turned inside out—She manipulates industriously every hem of the garments which passes through her bony fingers, and then dismisses her victims with some insulting remark about rebellion and secession.

The "Mrs. John Brown" may have been theatrically invented, but the reality of strip searches certainly sobered most Southern ladies.

Cordelia Scales, on her plantation eight miles north of Holly Springs, Mississippi, reported a visit from the Kansas Jayhawkers (anti-slavery guerrillas): "They tore the ear rings out of ladies ears, pulled their rings & breast pins off, took them by the hair; threw them down & knocked them about. One of them sent me word that they shot ladies as well as men & if I did not stop talking to them so & displaying my confederate flag, he'd blow my brains out." Amanda Worthington, also on a Mississippi plantation, told of the twenty thousand bales of government cotton that went up in flames, with more than a thousand head of cattle, a thousand head of hogs, and ten thousand bushels of corn lost to pillaging Yankees.

As Sarah Huff of northern Georgia remembered, "Yankees stripped us bare of everything to eat; drove off all the cattle, mules, horses; killed chickens; and turned their horses into a wheat field so that what the horses could not eat was destroyed by trampling." Dolly Lunt recalled a similar siege at her home near Covington, Georgia. "But like demons they rush in!" she moaned. "My yards are full. To my smoke house, my dairy, pantry, kitchen, and cellar, like famished wolves they come, breaking locks and whatever is in their way."

Mary Stribling in Fort Royal, Virginia, was appalled at Yankee conduct: "They came into the house and searched it several times and stole various articles of female apparel for which it is impossible to imagine what purpose they could use them. . . . They threatened the girls with the worst treatment. They wrote all over the walls addressing the ladies as if they were writing a letter, they write low pieces of obscenity to which they signed Jeff Davis's name." Even today some plantation houses in South Carolina and other regions proudly display Yankee graffiti to preserve the defilement of their homes by soldiers who clearly weren't "gentlemen." Graffiti was a small problem compared to shelling. Ella Hard remembered hearing as a young child a

terrifying sound, "then another, but before the third came we were safely in Mama's arms."

Later in the war, when Yankee invaders neared Hard's South Carolina plantation, her mother sent off two slaves ("in which Mama had no confidence"), "then my frail mother, little auntie and I eight years old proceeded to bury our treasures." This account sounds familiar—indeed the letters and journals of the planter class are fairly evenly divided on the issue of slave loyalty and buried treasure. The bulk of plantation legends, mostly promoted after the war, portray slaves within the household as loyal family retainers; one woman confided that before the attack on Columbia, South Carolina, she hid a box of silver with her cook, thinking, "would these great champions of liberty, these advocates of general emancipation, touch the negroes trunks or chests?" In her case the ploy worked and the silver was saved.

Despite vigilant attempts to outwit Union soldiers, Southern women were often deeply shaken by their encounters with the enemy. Louisa Henry fled her plantation to retire to a cottage in the woods, where she hoped to reside undisturbed. But as the wife of a quartermaster, she was sought out by the bluecoats. She confided, "I was in *mortal* terror all the time they were here, the children were clinging to my skirts, crying fit to break their hearts which prevented some of the brutal set from *burning*

the house, so they told the negroes." The savagery of this torching policy prompted Henrietta Lee to write directly to Union commander
General David Hunter: "Your name will stand on history's pages as
the Hunter of weak women, and innocent children: the Hunter to
destroy defenseless villages and beautiful homes—to torture afresh the
agonized hearts of widows."

Not all contact with Yankees was as brutal and hellish as the majority of Confederate accounts would lead us to believe. Sallie Moore, a
Virginian, reported that when one woman was accompanying a Union
officer up her stairs during an inspection of her home, "suddenly a string
broke and a shower of spoons and forks came raining down the steps
from under her hoops." In this tense moment the soldier gallantly
stooped to help the woman retrieve her silver and then returned it to her.

In another moment of drama, Susan Olmsted reported that her
mother was in Savannah during Sherman's occupation, trying to cope
with her newborn son and the two-year-old Susan, assisted only by her
sister and an aged male slave. As Olmsted described the situation:

> There was a loud rapping at my Mother's door. She and my aunt
> were too frightened to answer, but as Daddy Chance was not
> there at that time they decided they must, as the rapping contin-
> ued and was becoming more loud. When they unlocked, then
> opened the door they found several Negro soldiers in the uniform
> of the Union Army. When asked what they wanted they replied
> they wanted food. As the two sisters were attempting to get them
> to leave, a young Yankee officer ran upon the porch, brandishing
> his sword and put the Negroes to flight, some of them tumbling
> over the railing in their haste. Then sheathing his sword and re-
> moving his hat, the young man introduced himself as Capt. Mess-
> more. In the conversation that followed he said he was looking
> for young Mrs. Charles Olmsted. My mother answered that she
> was Mrs. Charles Olmsted. The officer told her that he had been
> quartered at her mother's home when the army was in Milledge-
> ville, and that her mother had asked him to call, if and when they
> reached Savannah.

The Union officer kindly helped them to find a cow to feed the ail-
ing baby, who later died despite this assistance. Recollections such as
these demonstrate that the Civil War allowed for Union civility as well
as the Yankee "depravity" most often depicted in Confederate sources.

BEAUFORT, SOUTH CAROLINA, WHERE UNION TROOPS HELPED AFRICAN AMERICANS
TO ESTABLISH SELF-SUFFICIENT FARM COMMUNITIES ON ABANDONED LANDS
DURING THE WAR.

African-American testimony serves as a powerful counterpoint to the strongly anti-Yankee character of Confederate memories. Former slave Eliza Sparks of Virginia confided with special poignancy an encounter with a Yankee:

> I was nursin' my baby when I heard a gallopin', an' fo' I coud move here come de Yankees ridin' up. . . . The officer mought of been a general—he snap off his hat an bow low to me an' ast me ef dis was de way to Gloucester Ferry. Den he lean't over an' patted de baby on de haid an' ast what was its name. I told him it was Charlie, like his father. Den he ast, "Charlie what" an' I told him Charlie Sparks. Den he reach in his pocket an' pull out a copper an' say, "Well, you sure have a purty baby. Buy him something with this; an' thankee fo' de direction. Goodbye, Mrs. Sparks." Now what you think of dat? Dey all call me "Mrs. Sparks!"

Beyond the battle of the recollections, it is important to recognize that war always elicits extreme brutalities. There is no question that

Union soldiers committed acts of terrorism, and many behaved brutally toward civilians. Hundreds of these activities appear in the public record and in private papers of Confederate civilians, and many are confirmed by African-American accounts. Nora Canning, a white woman in Macon, Georgia, reported that her missing husband was brought home after several days of torture by Yankees. He had been strung up by a rope and fell in and out of consciousness as he was raised and lowered. When the Northerners' demands for gold were met by consistent denials, Canning was finally released, after he had nearly choked to death. Scores of other Confederate civilians reported "ruffianism" during Yankee invasions, and many incidents did not end so happily. On September 19, 1863, a Raleigh paper reported: "Mrs. M. R. Fort was a lady sixty-five years of age, of the highest respectability and supposed to be worth some forty-thousand dollars. Yankees invaded her home with 'a gang of negroes' to the house at 2 o'clock a.m., took her out of bed and whipped her until 6 o'clock— four hours—to make her tell where her money could be found.—She

EMANCIPATION SCENE. THE EMOTIONAL, STYLIZED IMAGES OF THE ABOLITIONIST MOVEMENT, A MINORITY WITHIN ANTEBELLUM AMERICA, WERE ADOPTED AS POPULAR SYMBOLS OF NORTHERN SENTIMENT DURING WARTIME.

had no money, and of course could not satisfy the savages. The wretched lady died under the torture of the lash."

War was full of particular dangers for women, none more feared than rape—or, as white Southerners styled it, "dishonor infinitely worse than death." Evidence suggests that in this, as in other sexual matters, double standards abounded. Rape was a frequent byproduct of slavery, a violent act preserved by several African-American memoirs. The exaltation of white women's status was founded on a bedrock of female chastity, and it was a fundamental tenet of antebellum culture that ladies were pure uncompromised repositories of Southern virtue. Vices were left to white men only. Indeed, their transgressions with females of color were not tabulated on any register of moral error, outside the bitter recriminations that such illicit sexual relations fostered in white family circles. Despite the festering of this unpleasantness within the big house, and the concomitant sorrows in the slave cabins,

---

A PHOTOGRAPH OF ONE OF THE SCORES OF AFRICAN-AMERICAN SOLDIERS WHO WERE FOUND GUILTY OF CAPITAL CRIMES WHILE SERVING IN THE UNION ARMY, AND, DISPROPORTIONATELY, SENTENCED TO HANG.

women—black and white—
were powerless to prevent
these dangerous liaisons.

When the Civil War
broke out, most soldiers who
left wives and daughters alone
on homesteads hoped that
their enemies might be ruled
by officers and gentlemen who
would uphold the strict military ban on sexual misconduct.
Both armies determined that
rape would result in court-
martial and convicted rapists
might be executed. Both Union
and Confederate judge advocates enforced this law, although exceptions were found

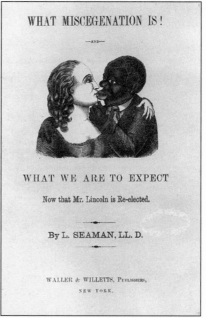

WHAT MISCEGENATION IS!

—AND—

WHAT WE ARE TO EXPECT

Now that Mr. Lincoln is Re-elected.

By L. SEAMAN, LL. D.

WALLER & WILLETTS, PUBLISHERS,
NEW YORK.

on both sides. Union justice appears to have been swift, merciless, and
not color blind: out of twenty-two executions for rape within the Union
Army, eleven were members of "colored regiments." Race, rank, status,
and other factors involving both the alleged victim and alleged perpe-
trator profoundly affected outcomes, but case files become murky and
complicated—we have only a very slim body of material, and little or
no research has been conducted on this topic.

The rapes of black women were publicly revealed in the Northern
press during this period, but their victims remained unnamed unless
they swore out a complaints against their attackers or sought legal
redress—which was extremely rare. Confederate accounts of rape are
few, black or white, although examples are found in the writings of
some physicians. Dr. Daniel Heywards Trezevant of Columbia, South
Carolina, described a vicious Yankee incursion full of murder and may-
hem, including "the case of Mr. Shane's old Negro woman, who after
being subjected to the most brutal indecency from seven of the Yankees, was, at the proposition of one of them to 'finish the old bitch' put
into a ditch and held under water until life was extinct." In a case of a
white victim of attempted rape, Trezevant uses initials to mask her

---

ABOVE: EMANCIPATION STIRRED UP FRENZIED ACCOUNTS OF INTERRACIAL SEX,
PROMOTING RACIST RESPONSE IN BOTH THE NORTH AND, ESPECIALLY, THE SOUTH.

identity. "Mrs. T.B.C. was seized by one of the soldiers, an officer, and dragged by the hair and forced to the floor for the purpose of sensual enjoyment," he wrote. "She resisted as far as practical—held up her young infant as a plea for sparing her and succeeded, but they took her maid, and in her presence, threw her on the floor and had connection with her." Both Trezevant and the abolitionist press were willing to use the rapes of black women as evidence, but each for their own purpose.

Trezevant identified only *black* Southern women as rape victims, with the sole exception of a woman who was driven insane by the experience. "Mrs. G. told me of a young lady about 16, Miss Kinsler, who . . . three officers brutally ravished and who became crazy from it," he wrote. While gang rape could and perhaps did result in a complete mental breakdown, propriety nevertheless dictated that any lady named in such a circumstance be banished from society.

Southern culture demanded a wall of silence around almost all sexual matters in the mixed company of men and women, a rule to which Southern matrons and belles universally subscribed. Only exceptional Southern white women even hinted at their fears or their experiences, among them Clara D. MacLean. In her postwar account, MacLean recounted one of the "last raids," when a Union soldier invaded her home on a farm in North Carolina. She had sewn her money into the side of her dress, but lied to the soldier about it. "'This is all the money I have in the world,' I said, holding up the sixpence, 'but you can have it if you wish.' He threw it aside with an impatient gesture and another oath and walked off. Before I was aware of his intention, he had locked the door. I rose and walked toward it. 'Come,' I said, 'and I will show you the trunks in the other room, as there is nothing here, you see, in the way of arms.' But he had stationed himself in front of the door, his back toward it. For a moment, nay, a long minute—centuries it seemed to me—we stood thus." But MacLean was able to bluff her way out of the room. She later shuddered as she watched the same man rip open the dress of another woman to find a handkerchief full of gold dollars.

These scenes of confrontation and danger were the plantation mistress' nightmare. Flight was prescribed in almost all cases if Confederate women were to be kept out of Yankee sights and certainly out of their hands. Refugee life had its ups, but mostly its downs. If women left they might escape the certainty of Yankee manhandling, but on the run they could trust little else. A refugee's life was harsh and challenging for well-heeled Confederates, and even more horrendous for the slaves forced to march along.

The adventures of Jane Pickett reflect the mixed emotions many Southern white women confronted during wartime disruptions. Pickett was born in 1816 and married in 1844; a childless couple, she and her husband lived on a large estate in Yazoo County, Mississippi, where they reared two nieces, Jessie and Lutie. When war broke out, the patriotic and industrious Jane Pickett closely followed the news. In January 1862 she wrote, "I attend to the cutting and making of negro clothes, giving out the wool and spinning it, knitting for the negroes, have an eye to the sick and expect to have weaving if the ports are not opened soon. All this keeps me busy, no time for reading except the news to see what those audacious Yankees are doing." Almost a year later she wrote, still from her home in Mississippi, "I love my country and have worked for our brave soldiers during the whole war." But it will not be long before she will be forced to leave, and she is grieved as her husband makes preparations. "It is a sad sight to see the tents made for us standing in the yard ready for us to fly before the face of the foe," Pickett added. "I heard the roar of canon this morning the enemy is constantly shelling our fortifications on the Yazoo. . . . But somehow, I am not alarmed. I dreamed last week the enemy overran the country and sold us all for slaves." Pickett claimed not to have been alarmed, but as her dream of being sold into slavery suggests, this was a world turning upside down.

Nearly six months later, after being forced to leave her home, Pickett confided her now bridled ambitions for her future, "We expect nothing more than a support for ourselves, and the few negroes we brought with us," she explains. "We have 35 in all, 19 refused to come with us or deserted on the road." Shortly thereafter she learns that her house was burned and all her remaining slaves have been liberated by Union troops. "If I could have my books and cabinet I could bear the loss very well—those were *my treasures,*" she lamented. "I have had so many bodily sorrows, that I do not weigh the loss of property in the scale against them, if I can have health, and enough to give me a little home and an humble independence." And she wryly noted: "Mr Pickett cannot bear so large a loss of property. As I never was exalted by prosperity, so I never could be debased by adversity." However, like many Southerners, she voiced legendary Confederate pride: "If the fortunes of war should threaten me with degradation *I am not compelled to live.*"

Pickett's life on the road is revealed in gripping letters to her mother. "Mississippi is almost depopulated of its black population, almost all going to Georgia or the Carolinas," she wrote. "Day after day droves of negroes and wagons, as well as the cares are passing through the country, some stop here, others go on to Georgia. South Western Georgia is thought will be a safe retreat as there are no government works near to invite Raids and the country is a poor one." Pickett and her family finally settled in Georgia in September 1863 and tried to re-establish themselves as planters. "Mr. Pickett says it will be hard to live without selling some negroes," she mentioned, "but he is going to carry all his back [to Mississippi] if we have to live on bread. We are comfortably situated here; live as well as could be expected on beef, bacon, flour, potatoes, vegetables of other kinds &c—we miss the milk & butter which is hard to get, supply not equal to demand. Our health is generally good though this place is now unusually sickly at this time. There is a funeral almost every day." Pickett was not willing to return home until Yankees were driven out of Mississippi, and so her husband rented seventy slaves in anticipation of leasing or buying a plantation in Georgia. The Picketts were not alone—dislocated Confederates across the region refused to give up the trappings of plantation life, preserving slavery at all cost.

The buffeting winds of war dispirited women throughout the Confederacy. Women were especially hard hit in the upper South, particularly Virginia, where Union troops constantly threatened. Fort Royal, Virginia, native, Lucy Buck reflected: "Separated from those dear members of our household by more than mere distance of miles— circumstances that might well preclude our ever hearing from them again. Our country run over by our remorseless foes—there we sat, completely in the power of our implacable enemies whom we were hourly expecting—enemies who would pillage and destroy our home, imprison or exile all our natural protectors and leave us poor females and children defenseless." Emma LeConte in South Carolina revealed her utter sense of defeat in February 1865 with the conquest of Columbia, "I ran upstairs to my bedroom window just in time to see the U.S. flag run up over the State House," she wrote. "O what a horrid sight! What a degradation! After four long bitter years of bloodshed and hatred, now to float there at last! That hateful symbol of despotism! I do not think I could possibly describe my feelings. I know I could not look at it." She then went on to describe: "The place is literally in ruins. The entire heart of the city is in ashes—only the outer edges remain." Yet LeConte vowed: "We have lost everything, but if all this—negroes—property— all could be given back a hundredfold I would not be willing to go back

REFUGEE FAMILY. THOUSANDS OF SOUTHERN FAMILIES WERE FORCED TO GATHER THEIR BELONGINGS AND HEAD FOR AN UNKNOWN DESTINATION IN ORDER TO ESCAPE UNION INVASION.

to them. I would rather endure any poverty than live under Yankee rule." The LeConte family, like many, debated the prospects of permanent exile, resettling abroad.

One of the most galling issues for many Confederates was the presence of black soldiers in the Union Army. The use of armed African-Americans in the South was a policy the Union army used deliberately to demoralize secessionists. It worked effectively in the case of Virginia McCollum Stinson, of Camden, Arkansas, who complained: "These were trying times to us, we were almost like prisoners in our own homes, but our faith in God was strong. Only one thing stirred my Southern blood to heat, was when a negro regiment passed my home going to fight our own dear men at Poison Springs [the battle on April 18, 1864]. How fierce they did look, it was then that I gave vent to my feelings." In Orange County, Virginia, Mary Wall also expressed her ire. "Well, in truth, I think it would be provocation sufficient to arouse the temper and indignation of every one who was born and reared on southern soil, to be halted by a negro sentinel; who that is not dead to every sense of honor & humanity will submit to any such thing as negro equality; in the sunny south we cannot, we will not."

White Southern women were also vehemently opposed to Union

WHITE SOUTHERNERS PROMOTED IMAGES OF RACIAL HARMONY, WITH ROMANTICIZED PORTRAITS SUCH AS THESE.

soldiers keeping company with African-American women. For example, Fanny Andrews, daughter of a prominent Georgia judge, disapproved of Federal soldiers strolling in the District of Columbia with "black creatures" on their arms. Georgia plantation mistress Ella Gertrude Clanton Thomas composed a vindictive letter to Mrs. William T. Sherman, claiming that the Union general was living with a black woman Thomas referred to as "Sherman's wife," but added that Mrs. Sherman should not be insulted because it was a general practice among Yankee officers. (The letter was never sent.)

This vicious rhetoric about African-American women was nothing new. But the fact that many planter-class women were cast into closer contact with black women during the war was certainly new. More than ever, they were forced into dependent relationships from which one might suppose intimacy might naturally flow. Narcissa Black of McNair County, Tennessee, described interracial quilting parties in her wartime letters, recalling evenings that lasted past midnight with twenty or more women involved. But Black's is a rare account of socializing across the color line, and she did not live in plantation country.

Reports of blacks and whites banding together against Yankee incursion cannot be translated into any genuine breakdown of racial segregation. Whatever dislocations transpired, blacks remained without any real standing within the Confederacy, a nation premised on white supremacy. To assume that wartime created any genuine blurring of the color line seems reckless speculation, or, worse, the acceptance of romanticized recollections. Many white memoirs, penned entirely after war's end, fondly celebrated black loyalty. However, during the prolonged struggle, few whites could afford to question blacks' wartime loyalties, even if they had thought to solicit slaves' opinions. And what would blacks have been at liberty to reply, but an echo of the slaveowner's assumptions of shared concerns? Postwar testimony from African Americans differs dramatically from white Confederate accounts and reinforces the notion that former slaveowners shaped their recollections to suit political purposes. Our reconstructions today can provide only partial revelations.

Well into the conflict, tragedy and jubilation, patriotism and self-preservation, commingled among both black and white with swift and disruptive abandon. Families were unmanned and scattered, children were orphaned, and many were born to fathers long buried. The joy of weddings and christenings were twisted into grief as the rituals of births and marriage gave way to harrowing attempts at survival. A pall spread over the Confederacy. White women and men realized that their victory, if it ever came at all, would be preceded by a protracted drain of human and material resources while blacks became acutely aware that the real battle would begin after soldiers lay down their arms.

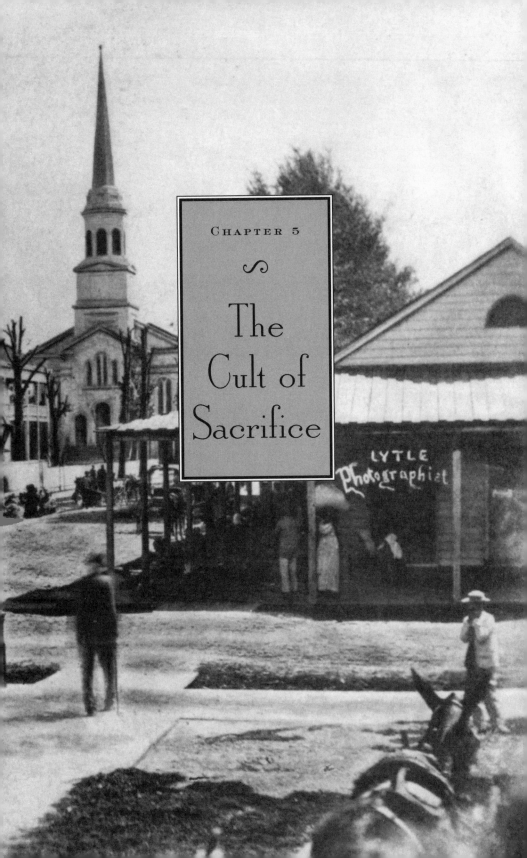

CHAPTER 5

The
Cult of
Sacrifice

LYTLE
Photographist

The Cult of Sacrifice

A t a gathering of Confederate war veterans in Richmond in 1888, the former South Carolina senator and decorated war hero General M. C. Butler proclaimed: "Do the annals of any country or of any period furnish higher proofs of self-sacrificing courage, self-abnegation and more steadfast devotion than was exercised by Southern women during the whole progress of our desperate struggle. . . . The sufferings of men . . . were mild inconveniences when compared with the anguish of soul suffered by the women at home, and yet they bore it all with surpassing heroism."

The recognition of women's "surpassing heroism" can be seen as valorization of female efforts, but the description of men's sufferings as "mild inconveniences" shows the obsessive hyperbole that Southern womanhood elicited. The glorification and embellishment of women's role within wartime was an article of Confederate faith that has only recently faced secular scrutiny.

The launching of the legends began almost as soon as the guns were fired at Fort Sumter. White women's staunch support, crucial to gearing up men for this role in battle, could blunt the effects of sacrifice made on the home front. Most women little understood how pronounced and prolonged these sacrifices might be when they gaily waved men off to war. To divert women's attention from the painful

Pages 136–37: Bread line in Baton Rouge.
Opposite: Detail of *The Burial of Latane* (1864). When this painting was first displayed in Richmond, patriots dropped coins in a bucket in front of it. Lithographs after the work found their way into thousands of Southern homes after the war.

CONFEDERATE VETERANS' REUNION.

realities that would too shortly dawn on them, and to inspire them in the struggle, the Confederate press and government rarely missed the opportunity to feature women's "sacrifice." Plantation mistress Maria Louisa Fleet rallied her fellow countrywomen in a letter to the *Richmond Enquirer:* "Let us work for them with our needles as long as they defend us with their bayonets, and when our glorious cause triumphs, let us share with them the victory."

The question of sacrifice was uppermost in the minds of those who would fight. Many wealthy and influential men formed separate military units, drawing manpower from the slaveholding elite to demonstrate their willingness to share the burdens of war. A former governor of North Carolina donated five sons to the army and the list of wellborn planter aristocrats who sent off heirs to die in the war is endless. One family, the Bells of North Carolina, had twelve men in the same regiment; when one of them died in the battle at Fredericksburg, Virginia (December 11–15, 1862), he was the ninth to fall in battle. But even these sacrifices could not satisfy the insatiable war machine.

By September 1862 the Confederate Congress was forced to take such unpopular measures as raising the upper age limit for the draft to forty-five. The next month, it instituted the equally unpopular "twenty Negro law," allowing some slave owners and overseers exemption from service. Yet the privilege of military exemption did not guarantee comfort or safety to the master class.

The wartime birth of Southern matron Lee Meriwether stands as an example of the hardships faced by planter-class whites, and contributes further to the legend of General Sherman's inhumanity—although Sherman is but one (certainly the most infamous) of several Union commanders vilified in legends cherished by Confederate descendants. According to family folklore, when Sherman was military commander of Memphis in December 1862, while the city was still being shelled for recapture, he issued an edict stating that the wives of "Rebel officers" had twenty-four hours to depart the city or go to prison. Meriwether's mother paid a visit to Sherman, thinking that her advanced pregnancy would convince him to remove her name from the list. He allegedly replied, "I'm not interested in Rebel wives or Rebel brats; if you are in Memphis after tomorrow you will be kept in prison until the rebellion is crushed." The thought of this double confinement hurried the young mother home, where she piled blankets, clothes, and her two other children into a buggy and hitched it to a mule. Two weeks and more than 150 miles later, she stopped at a cottage in Columbus, Mississippi, to give birth to her daughter, Lee.

Many of the most poignant moments of sacrifice were satirized as well as sentimentalized by whites. To relieve the constant tension in the Confederacy, Southern wags took the opportunity to make light of deadly serious situations. When nearly twenty thousand citizens of New Orleans crowded a levee to bid farewell to Rebels expelled on February 20, 1863, a patriot wrote a poem lampooning the conduct of Union guards. The bluecoats tried to maintain order in the chaotic atmosphere at the pier, but the crowd jostled its way forward to bid the men farewell. When Union officers bellowed "stand back" to the oncoming throng, women pressed forward, waving with

ABOVE: *Women Dressed in Gay Colors*. This post-war illustration demonstrates the way in which African Americans were viewed as "picturesque decoration" for the Southern landscape — images that perpetuated myths in both North and South.

abandon. The Rebels dubbed this incident the "Pocket Handkerchief War" and Marion Southwood composed a mock epic, which included the following stanzas:

> In times to come, when lamps are lit
> And fires brightly blaze,
> While round the knees of heroes sit
> The young of happier days
>
> Who listen to their storied deed,
> To them sublimely grand—
> Then glory award its meed
> Of praise to Bank's [Union general] band
>
> And fame proclaim that they alone
> (In triumph's loudest note)
> May wear henceforth, for valor shown,
> A woman's petticoat.

The Seven Days battles (from June 26, 1862, at Mechanicsville, Virginia, to July 1 at nearby Malvern Hill) forced Union general George B. McClellan's retreat, enabling Confederate forces to save Richmond. But the Union defeat left twenty thousand Confederates dead or wounded. A poem that appeared in the *Charleston Courier* reveals the soberer side of wartime verse:

> Fold away all your bright-tinted dresses
> Turn the key on your jewels today,
> And the wealth of your tendril-like tresses
> Braid back, in a serious way.
> No more trifling in the boudoir or bower,
> But come with your soul in your faces
> To meet the stern needs of the hour!

Women's petticoats, mocked in the New Orlean's poem, also played a more serious role in the war effort. During the Seven Days battles, the federals launched balloons that allowed them critical observations, and Confederate general James Longstreet lamented the Union advantage. With no silk available to make a balloon, Longstreet sent out an urgent SOS to the countryside and gathered impressive results. Confederate women emptied their closets for the cause, and enough gowns were collected to construct a Rebel balloon. This marvelous patchwork contraption, which Longstreet called "the last silk dress in the Confederacy," significantly enhanced rebel military strategy. Unfortunately, the balloon was stored on a steamer docked on the James River that was captured by the Union navy. Again, this legend has a double meaning. While it provides telling insight into Confederate concepts of women's roles and contributions, it also exemplifies the way in which these exaggerated tales diminish as well as exalt women, in true chivalric fashion.

Wartime periodicals circulating in the South were always filled with hints of how women might show their sacrifice—not just warnings like the Charleston paper's "no more trifling in the boudoir" but advice, in both literature and letters to the editor. One woman in Mobile urged her peers to donate family jewels and silver "to assist in redeeming the currency of the Confederacy." Another Alabama woman, who signed herself as "Delilah, a Niece of James Madison," devised a radical scheme that involved all Confederate women selling their hair to European wigmakers and donating the profits to the government. She calculated that two million women could chop off two braids of hair each, which, sold at the going rate of twenty dollars a pair, would provide forty million dollars toward retiring the Confederate debt. She demanded that all females over the age of twelve heed her call: *"Let every patriotic woman's head be shingled . . . and even the vilest foe will stand abashed in her presence."* There is no evidence to indicate that this hair style caught on. More commonly, each individual sought her own path to Confederate sacrifice.

For one example, when Judith Brockenbrough McGuire, the

Above: Nora Fontaine Calhoun, a representative Confederate girl.

daughter of a Virginia Supreme Court judge and the mother of two soldiers, became a refugee from her Alexandria home, she deposited her two daughters safely in Mecklenburg County before securing a position with the commissary department in Richmond and taking on volunteer hospital duties. Reporting in the spring of 1863, her own account reflected scarcity everywhere in the unoccupied South. "Several of us are engaged in making soap, and selling it, to buy things which seem essential to our wardrobes," she wrote. "A lady who has been perfectly independent in her circumstances, finding it necessary to do something of the kind for her support, has been very successful in making pickles and catsups for restaurants." McGuire told tales from the Confederate capital of wretchedly poor women denied the dole, mothers seeking food for their children, and other sad sights.

The Confederate government was finding it difficult to deliver on its promises, and the threat of starvation loomed. As early as April 1863 Confederate authorities began to collect taxes in kind, its currency increasingly devalued while government stockpiles shrank. Planters, cash poor, began to pay the government with wool and cotton, used to clothe the armies. Mistresses feared that veterans' children, like too many soldiers themselves, would be barefoot by winter.

Children lost their childhood in the chaos and cruelty of war. Carrie Berry, a young white girl in Atlanta, remembered turning ten in 1864: "I did not have a cake. Times were too hard so I celebrated with ironing. I hope by my next birthday we will have peace in our land so that I can have a nice dinner." Emma LeConte was thirteen when the war broke out. At seventeen she wrote: "I have seen little of the light-

ABOVE: HAIR SCULPTURE OF A CRUCIFIX. BRAIDED HAIR WAS OFTEN WOVEN INTO MEMENTOS, MOST COMMONLY RINGS OR BRACELETS, FOR LOVED ONES. THIS ELABORATE PIECE IS INTRICATE AND UNUSUAL.

heartedness and exuberant joy that people talk about as the natural heritage of youth. It is a hard school to be bred up in and I often wonder if I will ever have my share of fun and happiness." Another girl confided, "I think the war is teaching us some useful lessons—we are learning to dispense with many things and to manufacture other." Self-reliance was an important part of maturing, but too many Confederate children moved without pause into adult experiences.

Cornelia Peake McDonald, forced to evacuate her home in Winchester, Virginia, early in the war, moved her bedraggled family from site to site to escape the Yankees. At one point, after spending her morning hiding valuables, smuggling chickens into garrets, and burying silver, she came upon her three-year-old, clutching her doll Fanny and sobbing, "The Yankees are coming to our house and they will take all our breakfast and will capture me and Fanny." McDonald's daughter was right to be worried, for children were not always spared in the melee of Yankee invasion. Another mother in Lancaster, South Carolina, recounted her daughter's ordeal at the hands of "Sherman's bummers":

> A lovely little girl of six years, who had treasured her pet doll and a cake of sweet soap, a great luxury in those days, during all her journey from Columbia [which had been recently burned], sprang out of bed, seized her treasures, and childlike darted under the bed for refuge. . . . One of the men approached the bed, and finding it warm, in a dreadful language accused us of harboring and concealing a wounded rebel, and swore he would have his heart's blood. He stooped to look under the bed, and seeing the little white figure crouching in a distant corner, caught her by one rosy little foot and dragged her forth. The child was too terror-stricken to cry, but clasped her little baby, and her soap, fast to the throbbing little heart. The man wrenched both from her and thrust the little one away with such violence that she fell against the bed.

McDonald provided another tale guaranteed to wet a sympathetic cheek with her account of the plight of a Confederate woman named Mrs. Lechter. Lechter was forced to house Yankee officers, but after the night's lodging the mistress's hospitality was repaid with arson. "When they rose from breakfast, one of them, Capt. Berry, informed Mrs. Lechter that he should immediately set fire to her home," wrote

CHILDREN WATCH SOLDIERS AT SUDLEY FORD, NOT FAR FROM THE SECOND
BATTLE OF BULL RUN IN MARCH 1862.

WOMAN WITH HER HORSE AT THE CHARLESTON MARKET. IN THE ANTEBELLUM
ERA IT HOUSED SLAVE AUCTIONS, BUT DURING THE WAR IT BECAME A PRODUCE AND
LIVESTOCK MARKET.

McDonald. "He took a bottle of benzine, or some flammable fluid, and pouring it on the sofas and curtains in the lower rooms, applied a match, and then proceeded up stairs. Mrs. Lechter ran up stairs and snatching her sleeping baby from the cradle, rushed from the house with it, leaving everything she had to the flames." McDonald arrived later to find "Mrs. Lechter sitting on a stone in the street with her baby on her lap sleeping and her other little children gathered around. She sat tearless and calm, but it was a pitiable group, sitting there with their burning house for a background to the picture." Another women recalled the vengeance exacted when an old woman named Mrs. Woody, who lived not far from Richmond, sassed federal authorities. Union troops kept landing their balloon near her yard and would tell her what they had seen. In disgust Mrs. Woody replied, "Yes, Moses also viewed the promised land, but he never entered." In a fit of pique, Union troops burned her church to the ground—perhaps their idea of a fitting response to her biblical allusion.

These legends of Union brutes—burning churches and terrorizing children of "rosy feet" and "throbbing heart"—are not in dispute. But the language and descriptions are so treacly and formulaic that they might be viewed as a genre designed to evoke pathos. This propagandistic "Lost Cause" style did not really come into vogue until the 1890s, but white Southerners began to hawk these literary wares even before surrender.

Many women unself-consciously betrayed their own ignorance by harping on indignities and sacrifices that contemporaries may find ludicrous. Amanda Worthington reported from her home in Washington County, Mississippi, that she suffered hardship when in June 1863, at the age of seventeen, "I had to stay here all by myself, not even a servant with me." We might be sympathetic to a girl who had been wholly abandoned, but it turns out that there were indeed other people in the house. Worthington is talking about being forced to sleep unattended by a slave. A child of privilege, she felt unprotected because "it was the first time in my life I had staid in a room wholly by myself." Margaret Junkin Preston, a Virginia writer, tried to wring a tear from her reader when she revealed in a letter dated February 29, 1864: "G. and H. at Sally White's birthday party: H. said they had 'white mush' on the table: on inquiry, I found out it was ice cream! Not having made any ice-cream since wartimes, the child had never seen any, and so called it white mush."

These deprivations pale considerably when contrasted with

another group of young people coerced into sacrifice: slave children. Systematically robbed of childhood and routinely removed from parents when very young, slave children found growing up a stressful and accelerated process during wartime. Many black youths on plantations initially found the idea of war exotic and intriguing. Rachel Harris recalled: "I went with the white chillun and watched the soldiers marchin'. The drums was playing and the next thing I heerd, the war was gwine on. You could hear the guns just as plain. The soldiers went by just in droves from soon of a mornin' til sundown." But soon, the depletion of adult labor increased the burdens on slave children. Henry Nelson, only ten years old when the war broke out, remembered later, "You know chillun them days, they make em do a man's work." Eliza Scantling, fifteen in 1865, remembered that she "plowed a mule an' a wild un at dat. Sometimes me hands get so cold I jes' cry."

For slave children the prospect of an invading enemy was confusing and at times terrifying. One slave remembered being told by the overseer when only ten years old that Yankees had "just one eye and dat right in de middle of the breast." So frightened was Mittie Freeman, also ten, that she hid in a tree when the first bluecoats arrived. Ample evidence demonstrates that in many instances black children overcame apprehensions and even became enamored of Union soldiers. Still, although they might empathize with the adults' jubilation over impending freedom, at the same time they were children, overwhelmed and frightened by the prospect of change. Additionally, carnage was close at hand, and many slave children witnessed its frightening results. James Goings, only three when war broke out, recalled that by the end of the struggle, "it wuzn't nuthin' to fin' a dead man in de woods."

Slave children made their unwilling offerings, too; indeed, many black children sacrificed parents to the terrible conflict. As slave men fled the plantations, leaving their families behind, thousands of children became fatherless and hundreds were orphaned. Former slave Amie Lumpkin of South Carolina recalled her wartime loss: "My daddy go 'way to de war 'bout dis time, and my mammy and me stay in our cabin alone. She cry and wonder where he be, if he is well or he be killed, and one day we hear he is dead. My mammy, too, pass in a short time."

Among whites, not all sacrifices were viewed morbidly at war's beginning. The cult of sacrifice began on a rather high note of camaraderie and fellowship. Parthenia Hague described, in a characteristically saccharine tone, the way in which women in the Alabama countryside would gather for spinning bees, with "as many as six or eight wheels . . . whirring at the same time." Hague was heartened by these efforts. "We were drawn together in a closer union, a tenderer feeling of humanity linking us all together, both rich and poor; from the princely planter, who could scarce get off his wide domains in a day's ride, and who could count his slaves by the thousand, down to the humble tenants of the log-cabin on rented or leased land."

An egalitarian spirit existed not just in rural areas but in towns and cities where people feeling "the pinch of war" would have "recourse occasionally to a contribution supper, or 'Dutch treat,'" as Richmond resident Constance Cary remarked. What "democratic feasts those were," she added, "where major-generals and 'high privates' met with equal footing."

Confederate housewives overnight were expected not only to tighten their budgets but to give up all sorts of necessary items, from food to medicine. Money was scarce, and some goods were not to be had at any price. Ironically, slave women took the lead and introduced mistresses to herbal remedies and folk medicines. Parthenia Hague reported that planter wives came up with some ingenious solutions when they took to the woods—"our drug stores" as she called them. Among other substitutes the women found were persimmons for dates, raspberry leaves for tea leaves, okra seeds for coffee beans, cottonseed oil for kerosene, and beeswax for candle wax (harking back to colonial times). She described one woman who took two bowls, put melted lard in them, and then floated two or three of the spiny ball-shaped fruits from a sweet gum tree, "which soon, becoming thoroughly saturated with the melted lard, gave a fairylike light, floating round in the shallow vessels of oil like stars."

The tone of these and other tales reveals a strong romantic theme meant to evoke pathos. Louisa McCord Smythe, in an unpublished manuscript, recalled her mother trying to keep flowers tended, a luxury that memorialized her dead son, Cheves, who had loved her gardens. Cheves McCord was worshiped by the family as an exemplar of Confederate sacrifice. His sister confided, "I have a letter from my brother to my mother thanking her for a supply of Quinine she had sent him, but saying that it would be impossible for him to take it as there was not enough for all, and he was not willing to take less risks than the men did." McCord did not die of fever—for which the quinine was sent—but from a head injury inflicted on the battlefield.

McCord's womenfolk tended the gardens abandoned by this fallen hero and kept the greenhouses warm against encroaching winter, but to no avail. In an elaborate recollection, a McCord slave, Tom, forlornly reported that the coal supply was gone and "with the scarcity of men and horses it was hard to get wood." The faithful retainer took great pains to tell the mistress that "he only had enough coal for one more fire." Smythe recalled: "The fire was lit but burned out before morning, and in a day or two our dear flowers were nothing but blackened sticks. The doors of the two greenhouses were locked and we left them like graves." It is the self-deception of memoir that allowed Smythe to dwell on the flowers rather than the family members who might freeze. The McCords bundled themselves in shawls against the chill but seemed impervious to the notion that they should have reserved their coal to warm themselves and their slaves rather than the family greenhouse.

The search for necessities preoccupied most Southern wives. One matron complained, "Slowly but surely the South was 'bled white.' Luxuries, there were none." As one girl in Winchester, Virginia, reported, "Out shopping all morning. I'd give a cent if Jennie Baker would quit sending for me to buy things for her. Its the bane of my existence for every store here in town is bare and nothing you want in there. Here today I walked all over town and couldn't get anything I wanted."

Pooling resources may have seemed a game of festive ritual early in the war, but by 1862 scarcity was worrisome, and by the summer of 1863, inflation and rationing made putting food on the table a major ordeal. In the summer of 1863 Lucy Johnston Ambler fretted: "Indeed everything looks very gloomy. From having a comfortable table, I am reduced to bacon bone. . . . I have a very sick grandchild and several

---

ABOVE: A CHILD'S TINY PORTRAIT IN A CIVIL WAR ERA LOCKET. MANY SUCH MEMENTOS WERE FOUND UNCLAIMED ON BATTLEFIELDS.

servants sick with no suitable medicine." Louisa McCord Smythe described conditions in Charleston shortly before federal occupation: "Food was frightfully scarce and what there was was of the coarsest description. Bacon, cornbread made with just salt and water, and biscuits made of the wheat ground up whole, very coarse and always with only salt and water to mix them, were the staples, in fact the only supplies of the table. Wagons were sent from Georgia with provisions which the town distributed to those who came for them. For hours there would be a crowd of the best sort of people, standing in line for their chance for a little bit of something." Smythe recalled that she felt faint while waiting in line and had to return home—perhaps empty-handed but not deprived, since she made her slave stay behind to collect her rations.

Even as difficulties mounted, plantation women were expected to carry on with total restraint and without complaint. An Atlanta matron proclaimed: "I knew women to walk twenty miles for a half bushel of coarse, musty meal with which to feed their starving little ones, and leave the impress of their feet in blood on the stones of the wayside ere they reached home again. When there, the meal was

WOMEN LEFT BEHIND BY HUSBANDS IN THE ARMY OFTEN SUFFERED
ENORMOUS DEPRIVATION.

THE SOLDIER'S WIFE

cooked and ravenously eaten, though there was not even salt to be eaten with it. Yet these women did not complain, but wrote cheerful letters to their husbands and sons, if they were yet living, bidding them to do their duty and hold the last trench." Is it any wonder that Atlanta became such a font for Confederate legends?

Women's sacrificial courage was summarized by Smythe's declaration: "We would have died before we would complain to a man in the army. They had enough to bear without that." But after several seasons of war, no amount of sanitizing the truth could prevent soldiers from knowing of the dire straits on the Confederate home front.

One woman who confronted the price of seventy dollars a barrel for flour exclaimed: "My God! How can I pay such prices? I have seven children; what shall I do?" She encountered a callous merchant who replied, "I don't know, madam, unless you eat your children." Starving Confederates did not revert to cannibalism, but they were willing to seize supplies hoarded by unscrupulous speculators. In April 1863 an Atlanta proprietor refused to lower the price of bacon, inspiring an angry veteran's wife to draw a pistol and allow her fellow women shoppers to "liberate" food supplies valued at over two hundred dollars. Instead of calling the police, witnesses to the theft went to the press to solicit funds to distribute to indigent wives of soldiers. Donations and applications were channeled through the offices of Atlanta's *Intelligencer.*

The looting of Confederate storerooms was increasingly a problem as the war went on, especially in the border states and in interior North Carolina and Tennessee, where mountain folk were divided bitterly over the war effort and guerrilla warfare was common. Despite divisions of loyalty, all Southerners were in agreement that poor harvests, the blockade, and shortages made their lives miserable. The Union campaign of starving out the Rebels was beginning to wreak havoc.

Salt, necessary for baking and for curing meats, was especially crucial. Susan Bradford, blockaded in Florida, described the saltworks her father established: "A white foam comes at first and then the dirtiest scum you ever saw bubbles and dances over the surface, as the water boils away it seems to get thicker and thicker, at last only a wet mass of what looks like sand remains. This they spread on smooth oaken planks to dry. In bright weather the sun does the rest of the work of evaporation, but if the weather is bad, fires are made just outside of a long, low shelter, where the planks are placed on blocks of wood. . . . It is very troublesome and it takes nine men to do the work." Bradford added that the entire operation, within range of Yankee gunboats, was in constant jeopardy.

The legendary stoicism Confederate women were expected to demonstrate was tested considerably by wartime hardship. Patience and restraint could and did falter in the face of impending doom. The constant cry for salt and bread echoed from the banks of the Shenandoah to the Delta and boomeranged back to the Confederate capital. In the wake of civil disturbances, a woman in Richmond wrote to a friend on April 4, 1863, repeating the words she heard a young girl say. "We are starving," the child is reported to have declared. "As soon as enough of us get together we are going to the bakeries and each of us will take a loaf of bread. That is little enough for the government to give us after it has taken all our men." According to the letter nearly a thousand of Richmond's women and children banded together and "marched along silently and in order." They methodically emptied stores of goods and refused to stop even when the mayor confronted them to "read the Riot Act." The mob even ignored the city battalion, and finally, in desperation, Jefferson Davis appeared. The Confederate president was at first greeted with hisses, "but after he had spoken some little time with great kindness and sympathy, the women quietly moved on, taking their food with them." Still, more than forty-eight hours later, an observer reported, "women and children are still standing in the streets, demanding food, and the government is issuing to them rations of rice."

All of northern Virginia, alarmed by the Richmond bread riot, spread the report. One woman confided to a friend, "I am telling you of it because not one word has been said in the newspapers about it." People throughout the countryside certainly understood the impulse that led to the riot, even if they disapproved. Virginia Cloud of Fort Royal, Virginia, complained: "I do not think the speculative spirit, so prevalent, is at all *patriotic*. I fear there are many who love *mammon* more than their country." Evidence of widespread scapegoating during this period also exists, with Jewish merchants in the Confederate capital targeted by unhappy civilians.

Government censorship suppressed news of such disturbances, but similar incidents erupted spontaneously throughout the South. In the winter of 1863 a shopkeeper in Macon, Georgia, was forced to negotiate with a crowd of women carrying brooms and brandishing fishing poles to protest the high price of meat. The town's mayor was unable to get the women to disperse, and indeed they reassembled the next day until

he pledged to distribute food supplies to needy families. In Marshall, North Carolina, rebel deserters broke into a government warehouse to obtain salt and even raided the house of a Confederate colonel. This set in motion a series of events that led to vicious reprisals and the Shelton Laurel massacre, in which over a dozen suspected of a guerilla raid were captured and then taken out and shot, including a sixty-year-old grandfather and a thirteen-year-old boy.

Feeding the Confederacy and keeping the economy going was an increasingly impossible task. Cotton was no longer king, and plantation mistresses were dangerously ignorant of the plunging value of this crop. Melissa Fouche in South Carolina reported her mother's dilemma: "She came down with the expectation of selling her cotton, but could not find a buyer." Without food, without money, many women were perilously close to the abyss.

Sarah Rice Pryor, a refugee outside Petersburg, Virginia, gave birth in a blizzard during Christmas 1863. Mother and newborn were still bedridden three months later when Pryor's furloughed husband sought out his family and found his wife and three children abandoned by their slaves and being cared for by a hired hand. The shocked husband then sold goods to raise three hundred dollars in gold, instructing his wife to "prepare a girdle to be worn all the time around [her] waist, concealed by [her] gown." Sarah Rice Pryor described the result: "The coins were quilted in; each had a separate section to itself so that with scissors I might extract one at a time without disturbing the rest." It was his desire that she never "again fall into the sad plight in which he had found me."

From the war's opening hours on through to the end, Confederates employed dramatic religious rhetoric to describe their plight. They were crusaders, holding their banners high against the heathen. Oratory and imagery were strewn with biblical oratory. But when their holy war was almost over, many wondered, like Christ on the Cross, why they had been forsaken. A girl wrote to her cousin from South Carolina: "This is indeed a terrible war. How many hearts have been made desolate by its ravages. How many vacant places around the family altars. How terrible is the wrath of God, our sins as a people has brought this upon us and we should humble ourselves before Him. I believe that Genl. Jackson was taken from us because we were making a god of him, not for any sin or unrighteousness in him, for I believe that he was not only doing good work as a soldier of our Confederacy but also of the cross." General Stonewall Jackson was indeed worshiped and revered during his military career. In death he became a martyr, and after the war he was canonized as part of the Confederate trinity: Davis, Lee, and Jackson.

Christian faith gave Confederate women their redemption as well. They struggled mightily to find some sense to the slaughter and to the endless drumbeat of defeat. A Virginia girl wrote to her sister shortly before the surrender, "And since the destruction of my own heart treasures (which now appears so long ago that it almost seems like a myth), I am thankful that I have been enabled to regard those wretched Yankee miscreants as only the rod of his paternal chastisement to draw us nearer to Himself."

A Georgia girl, Eliza Andrews, after a visit to Andersonville Prison where hundreds of Yankee prisoners had died, worried about vengeance: "I am afraid that God will suffer some terrible retribution to fall upon us for letting such things happen. If Yankees ever should come to South-West, Ga. . . . and see the graves there, god have mercy on the land." This prophecy of doom was perhaps realized in the form of William T. Sherman. When the Union general's troops set off from Atlanta to Savannah, the men proceeded in an orderly fashion, especially during the first ten days when they covered 275 miles. But after they reached Camp Lawton, a prisoner-of-war camp at Millen,

Georgia, many of the lawless brutalities emerged that made this campaign infamous. In face of the brutality, almost all white Southerners recast Sherman's march as God's test of their own faith.

Another severe test came for many Confederates during the Union's prolonged campaign for the control of Vicksburg, Mississippi, when thousands were caught up in the battle over this key port. This city on a bluff overlooking the Mississippi River had been the focus of federal military strategy for months. Union general Ulysses S. Grant finally gathered seventy thousand soldiers there to assault the Confederate force of twenty-eight thousand in the summer of 1863. Before surrender, the besieged Confederates would be reduced to eating horses, dogs, and rats. The bombardment was so fierce that civilians dug caves into the mountainside for shelter. The memoir of Mary Ann Loughborough gives ample testimony of the genuine hardships endured. She recalled an incident when a shell was lobbed into the center of a cave crowded with families. "Our eyes were fastened upon it, while we expected every moment the terrific explosion would ensue," she wrote. "I pressed my child closer to my heart and drew nearer the wall. Our fate seemed almost certain; and thus we remained for a moment with our eyes fixed in terror on the missile of death, when George, the servant boy rushed forward, seized the shell, and threw it into the street, running swiftly in the opposite direction." George and the cave dwellers escaped injury.

Nerves frayed, supplies disappeared, and the determined Yanks maintained their attack. Yet in May 1863, Confederates still kept up their spirits, singing about the siege in a parody of the popular song "Mocking Bird":

> *Twas at the siege of Vicksburg,*
> *Of Vicksburg, of Vicksburg—*
> *Twas at the siege of Vicksburg,*
> *When the Parrott shells were whistling through the air*
>
> *Listen to the Parrot shells—*
> *Listen to the Parrot shells:*
> *The Parrot shells are whistling through the air.*

Songs were weak ammunition against scurvy, rat-catching, and bombardment. Wounded animals limped around looking for grass and evading butchers. Nightly shelling kept frightened children awake.

JEFF DAVIS REAPING THE HARVEST.

THE YANKEE PRESS VILIFIED JEFFERSON DAVIS, CHARACTERIZED HERE AS A
GRIM REAPER IN *HARPER'S WEEKLY*.

The challenges were tremendous and daily life was precarious at best. Loughborough recalled a particularly awful day when one of the young girls, bored by confinement, ventured out. "On returning, an explosion sounded near her—one wild scream and she ran into her mother's presence, sinking like a wounded dove, the life blood flowing over the light summer dress in crimson ripples from a death wound in her side caused by the shell fragment. A fragment had also struck and broke the arm of a little boy playing near the mouth of his mother's cave." She recalled the frequency with which she heard the heartwrenching "moans of a mother for her dead child."

After countless deaths, the Confederates hoisted the white flag over Vicksburg on July 4, 1863. The soldiers were placated somewhat by the dignity they were accorded. As the skeletal figures stacked their arms, witnesses detected sympathy from Union conquerors. The treaty, concluded on a federal holiday, contained generous terms and nearly all soldiers were paroled.

The defeat at Vicksburg and almost simultaneous Union victory at Gettysburg (with fifteen thousand casualties out of the sixty thousand men engaged) seemed a dress rehearsal for the final surrender at Appomattox in April 1865. By this fateful time, many women saw doom on the horizon and began, consciously or unconsciously, to contemplate surrender. They continued to consolidate their own position as women worthy of Greek tragedy, an identity made explicit in Augusta Jane Evans's wartime novel *Macaria: or, Altars of Sacrifice* (1864).

Between these two historic moments—from this turning point in July 1863 to the treaty at Appomattox on April 9, 1865—thousands became refugees, hundreds of thousands were wounded, and tens of thousands were buried. Women could perhaps no longer suffer in silence and began to ask, as one South Carolinian did, "The great battles seem to move the Nation, but O! at what a cost—when shall the last be fought?" As they hoped and prayed for the final battle, few could contemplate life beyond war's end, afraid to anticipate the outcome.

CHAPTER 6

After
Appomattox

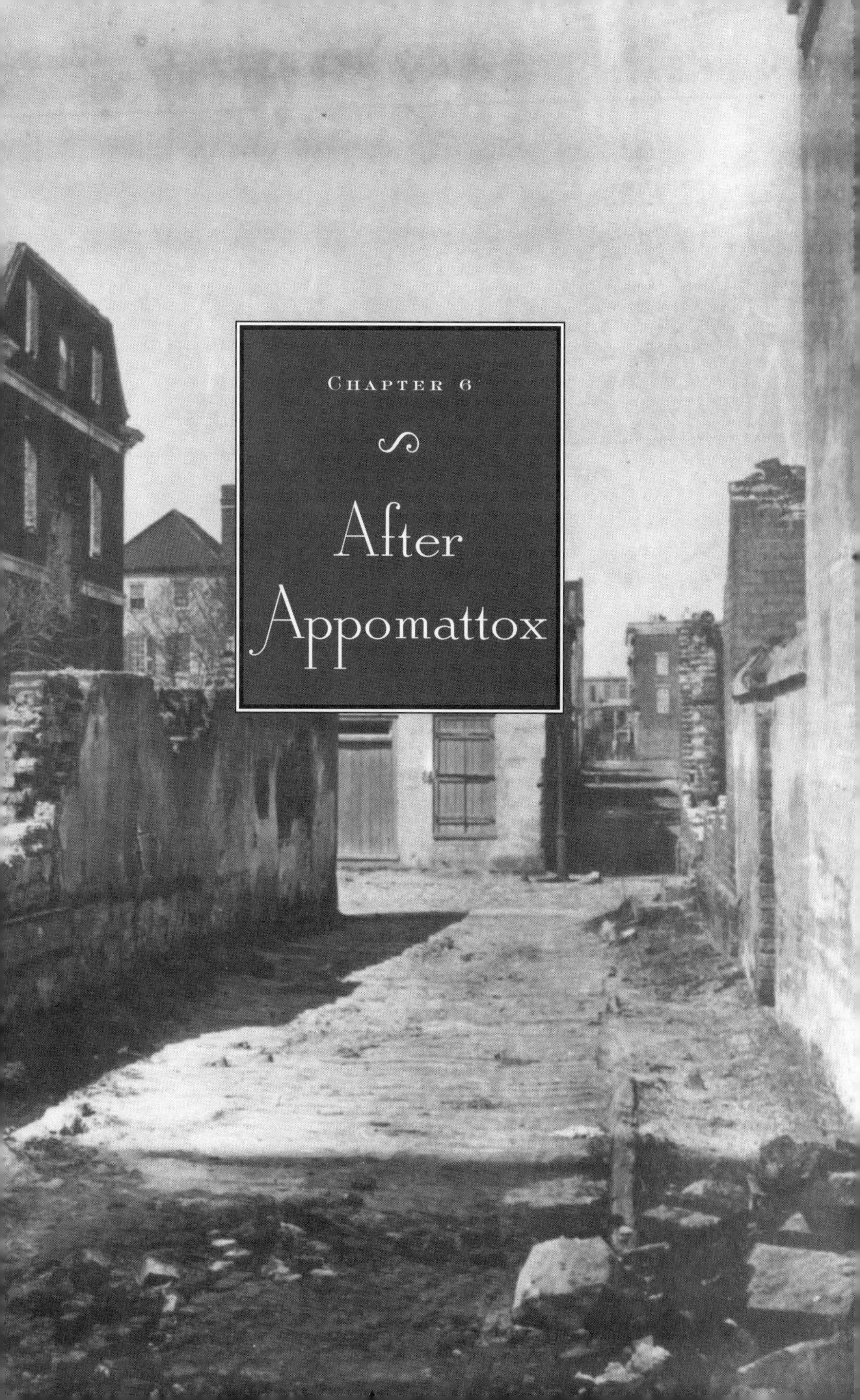

After Appomattox

When General Robert E. Lee surrendered his Army of Northern Virginia (twenty-six thousand troops) to General Ulysses S. Grant on April 9, 1865, at Appomattox, Southerners were shocked. Although Confederate president Jefferson Davis had fled the conquered capital of Richmond the week before, many were still unprepared for Lee's capitulation and those that rapidly followed: General Joseph Johnston's surrender in North Carolina on April 26, President Davis's capture in Georgia on May 10, and General Edmund Kirby-Smith's May 26 surrender of the Confederate armies west of the Mississippi. Within the short space of a month, the Confederacy became a conquered people.

Even after their own prolonged and bitter struggle, Confederate matrons were again expected to lighten the burdens of the defeated, long-suffering soldiers. Young women had to make good on their wartime promises, among them a debutante's claim that "I had rather take to my heart a private soldier who had returned from the war maimed and penniless than the coldblooded speculator who had grown rich, or the perfumed fop of hereditary wealth who had nursed his mustache at home, while their betters were bleeding in my defense, and in the defense of all that is worth living for—my country and her independence." Many men did indeed come home maimed and wounded, psychically as well as physically scarred by combat.

VIVIEN LEIGH AS SCARLETT BEFORE THE WAR: THE PERFECT IMAGE OF THE SOUTHERN BELLE IN HER PRISTINE ANTEBELLUM SPLENDOR.

To add to Confederate despair, African Americans jubilantly joined the North in celebrating Union victory, a celebration considerably muted by President Abraham Lincoln's assassination on April 14, 1865. Mathilda Dunbar, mother of author Paul Laurence Dunbar, recounted her memory of Union victory to a Works Progress Administration (WPA) interviewer during the 1930s. "I was in the kitchen getting breakfast," she recalled. "The word came—'All darkies are free.' I never finished that breakfast. I ran 'round and 'round the kitchen, hitting my head against the wall, clapping my hands and crying 'Freedom! freedom! freedom! Rejoice, freedom has come!'" Many African-American women, emancipated from tyrannical mistresses, flaunted their freedom in ways calculated to offend former owners. Women in the Jones family of Liberty County, Georgia, complained that freedwomen paraded in finery looted from white closets. One freed slave remembered with exasperation his wife's demand that their former mistress's four-poster bed be dragged into their cabin, even though the massive piece occupied the entire space. As a symbol of her liberation, she would sleep in the bed she had made for someone else most of her life. Many black laundresses in the aftermath of war refused the demeaning chores slavery had required and told plantation

VIVIEN LEIGH AS SCARLETT TRANSFORMED BY WAR: A VIVID IMAGE OF
BEDRAGGLED HARDSHIP.

women to soak and clean their own menstrual rags, for as freedwomen
they were unwilling to perform such labor.

Slavery was abolished with the passage of the Thirteenth Amendment
in December 1865, and the Fourteenth Amendment ratified in July
1868 extended citizenship rights to individuals of the former slave class,
though it granted the vote only to males. Voting rights were reinforced
and guaranteed by the Fifteenth Amendment, passed in 1868, and ratified in 1870. By federal statute, freedpeople were guaranteed civil
rights, including the right to work, to marry, to travel freely, and other

basic privileges. But the legislative improvement did little to ameliorate race relations during the crushing social and political upheaval during Reconstruction (1863–77).

The defeated Confederates reeled from the consequences of their failed rebellion. First they dealt with the dramatic and immediate results of war—including the loss of men. During the war years, the gender ratio had changed dramatically: The 1870 census counted thirty-six thousand more women than men in Georgia and twenty-five thousand more in North Carolina. In Atlanta more than eight thousand families, many headed by women, were reported to be utterly destitute in the wake of war. Expectations for women shifted dramatically as a generation of marriageable white women, struggling to meet the challenges of an occupied South, was forced into economic self-sufficiency.

Federal troops, a presence that did not disappear fully until the late 1870s, were a constant visible reminder of the Confederate failure. Many white Southern women railed against Union watchdogs, carrying on the wartime tradition of detestation and protest. Georgian Fanny Andrews reported that women pulled their drapes as if in mourning and avoided all contact with Union soldiers. In Macon, Wesleyan College students were forbidden to take evening walks for fear of encounters with Union soldiers. All over the South, white women boycotted social functions at which federal soldiers might appear. Myrta Lockett Avary claimed: "Any where in the land, a Southern girl's showing partiality for Federal beaux came under the ban. If there were nothing else against it, such a course appeared neither true, nor dignified; if it were not treason to our lost Confederacy, it were treason to our own poor boys in gray to flutter over prosperous conquerors."

ABOVE: A CONFEDERATE HERO WHO HAD LOST A FOOT.

Hanover, an antebellum homestead, in the post-war era. African Americans moved into the abandoned homes of former masters.

Food shortages created dire straits for former Confederates in the post-war South. Northern rations often kept starvation at bay.

ALABAMIANS RECEIVING RATIONS.—[Sketched by A. R. Waud.]

This ban was rigid and absolute during Reconstruction, but during the 1880s and on into the next century the feud between the gray and the blue became legendary. Jefferson Davis's own daughter, Varina (Winnie), born in 1864, experienced the brunt of this feud. Nicknamed "the Daughter of the Confederacy" despite the fact that she spent most of her early years abroad, Winnie Davis endeavored to fulfill this symbolic role, addressing veterans and dedicating memorials to please her parents. During the 1880s when she fell in love with Northerner Alfred Wilkinson, Jr., the grandson of an abolitionist, former Confederates were scandalized. Her parents forced her to break off the engagement, and she never married. A Shirley Temple vehicle called *The Littlest Rebel* (1936) sentimentalizes this legacy of star-crossed lovers in the postbellum era. Nevertheless "Yankee" remained a Southern epithet throughout most of the nineteenth century and into the twentieth, enjoying a dramatic revival during the civil rights struggles of the 1960s, which mirrored the bitterness of the 1860s.

Louisa McCord Smythe, a member of a prominent Charleston family, was outraged by postwar developments. On May 28, 1865, she described the occupation in a sarcastic rage: "We have one of the dear creatures [federal soldiers] posted at our corner where we have to see him whenever we leave the gate. It is too perfectly disgusting. . . . We were rather afraid to go to church today lest the Yankees might be dictating prayers to us." By June she wrote: "Oh dear! What is to become of our poor country! . . . Here we are having Yankee, Yankee, yankee, White Yankee & nigger Yankee, till we are more disgusted with them than ever. It will be no country for any one to live in I am afraid."

Smythe, like other aristocratic Southerners, dreamed of escape. "All I wish & long for is to get out of reach of it all just to go anywhere—Brazil, Australia, or anywhere else," she complained. "I believe we could be comparatively happy when once out of sight and hearing of these Yankees." Indeed the summer and fall of 1865 witnessed a Confederate exodus: Brazil and Mexico were two popular choices for colonists trying to re-establish the Confederate cause abroad, while England and France were popular destinations for disenchanted Southern emigrants. Confederate exiles created a large colony in Brazil, and Confederate customs are still celebrated there today. One Mexican experiment—the Carlotta colony, named after the wife of Mexican emperor Maximilian—failed as miserably as the Mexican "empire" this Austrian archduke, sent by Napoleon III, tried to establish. Similarly ill-conceived expeditions to British Honduras (Belize)

SHIRLEY TEMPLE IN *THE LITTLEST REBEL*, AT THE CENTER OF WHAT WAS SUPPOSED
TO BE ADORING ADMIRERS ON THE PLANTATION.

and Venezuela had little success. Hundreds also crossed the Canadian border as refugees, many, ironically, settling not far from where fugitive slaves had made their homes in the antebellum era.

But the vast majority of white Southerners did not leave the restored Union. The private papers of the planter class overflow with tales of poverty and harrowing woes in the postwar South. One alarmed Charleston aristocrat reported in September 1865: "Last evening about 8 o'clock, the bell of the house No. 35 Bogard Street was rung and upon the occupants repairing to the door to answer the call no person was to be seen, but a basket was discovered upon the steps. On taking the basket into the house, it was found to contain the living form of a white female babe, some two or three days old, with the following note pinned to its clothing: 'Will the lady of this house take this infant, as it was found in the street by a colored person, and take care of it the best she can, as I suppose it has not any mother. A FRIEND.' We are well aware that there have been great and important changes in the social and political relations at the South, but we never dreamt that nature had been so changed as to bring a human being into existence without a mother, and place them, too in the street." The needs of the region were so extreme that hundreds of Union relief organizations raised funds for the downtrodden South. The New York Ladies Relief Association was instrumental in this effort.

One Georgia woman, reporting on the Confederate plight, revealed that "the pinch of want is making itself felt more severely every day and we haven't the thought that we are suffering for our country that buoyed us up during the war. . . . There is nothing for us to do but bow our heads in the dust and let the hateful conquerors trample us under their feet." But Southern pride was only temporarily trampled, and the ladies of the so-called Lost Cause, those self-styled Confederate diehards, sought productive recourse. Many spent time and energy avoiding the dreaded Oath—a loyalty pledge that entailed renouncing the Confederacy as well as promising renewed devotion to the Union. The oath was required in order to receive rations, to participate in legal ceremonies such as weddings, and to restore citizenship.

With the South's terrible decline, which only worsened with Confederate surrender, one Lost Cause survivor confided white women "improvised a new social system in which absolute poverty, cheerfully borne, was the badge of respectability. Everybody was poor except the speculators." The conflicting demands of the new social order are vividly demonstrated in Lillian Hellman's drama *The Little Foxes,* in which families struggle over the question of prosperity in the New South.

The excess of indigent widows in the South, deprived of the generous pensions wives of Union veterans might obtain, created further economic instability. The governors of the Southern states were besieged by requests, many like the letter Mrs. A. G. Smith wrote in July 1866 to Governor James Orr of South Carolina. "I am a widow and before the war was in comfortable circumstances," she explained. "But from a too great trust in the Confederacy vested my capital in Confederate bonds and of course lost all in that way. . . . [having] inherited the proud spirit of my ancestors, it is very painful to me, to make this application and I have struggled hard to get along without doing so. At the same time, that I feel we are suffering from a common calamity and that hundreds of others, of the first respectability have been glad to accept aid from those benevolent societies who have done so much for our suffering South."

One Alabama man wrote to his brother in 1867: "You wish to know my plans. I do not know that I can claim just now to have any plans. . . . Our people are poor. I am at a loss to know what to do. If I can support my family, I shall be satisfied. I am not now doing that." Trying to resume regular operation of plantations was next to impossible. Most former slave owners resented their ex-slaves, and violent confrontations as well as severe havoc ensued.

Some planters did try to woo back freedmen to work for them. Colonel P. H. Anderson of Big Spring, Tennessee, wrote to a former slave in Ohio and received a lengthy response peppered with sarcasm, excerpts of which follow:

> I got your letter and was glad to find that you had not forgotten Jourdan and that you wanted me to come back and live with you again, promising to do better for me than anybody else can. . . . As to my freedom, which you say I can have, there is nothing to be gained on that score, as I got my free papers in 1864 from the Provost-Marshal-General of the Department of Nashville. Mandy says she would be afraid to go back without some proof that you were disposed to treat us justly and kindly; and we have concluded to test your sincerity by asking you to send us our wages for the time we served you. This will make us forget and forgive old scores, and rely on your justice and friendship in the future. I served you faithfully for thirty-two years, and Mandy twenty years. At twenty-five dollars a month for me, and two dollars a week for Mandy, our earnings would amount to eleven thousand six hundred and eighty dollars. Add to this the interest for the time our wages have been kept back, and deduct what you paid for our clothing, and three doctors visits to me, and pulling a tooth for Mandy and the balance will show what we are in justice entitled to. . . . Please state if there would be any safety for my Milly and Jane who are now grown up and both good looking.

OPPOSITE: JOHN ROGERS'S 1866 STATUE, *TAKING THE OATH AND DRAWING RATIONS*, SYMBOLIZED THE SURRENDER OF CONFEDERATE PRIDE.

You know how it was with poor Matilda and Catherine. I would rather stay here and starve—and die, if it come to that—than have my girls brought to same by the violence and wickedness of their young masters. . . . Say howdy to George Carter, and thank him for taking the pistol from you when you were shooting at me. . . . From your old servant Jourdan Anderson.

This ex-slave's frankness is quite unusual to find in correspondence, although perhaps not such an uncommon attitude on the part of many blacks after the Confederate defeat. Whites felt, nevertheless, wounded by the turn of events. A Kentucky plantation mistress wrote to her son: "All we had in the South is gone, all we owned in Louisville

FORMER SLAVE QUARTERS, FORT GEORGE, FLORIDA, REMAINED POST-WAR HOUSING FOR BLACKS, AS PHOTOGRAPHED IN THE 1870S.

NEGRO CHURCH. A RARE PHOTOGRAPH OF BLACKS IN THEIR OWN HOUSE OF WORSHIP.

lost—the negroes taken from us, so nothing remains but the land. From that we may get a living." The daughter of Fanny Kemble and Pierce Butler, Frances Butler Leigh tried to revive her family's Sea Island plantations, but was met with a reluctance on the part of her black employees to return to the old days. According to Leigh, African Americans began to call whites by their surnames without any title and refused to remove their hats when addressing whites. She further claimed that former slaves worked when they wanted and that many armed themselves. As a result, Leigh reported, some white women slept with pistols by their bedsides. In this atmosphere of mistrust, fear, and anger, some whites fled. Wealthy aristocrat Laura Comer sold all her property and moved North, choosing to live in exile rather than tolerate such conditions in her Georgia home.

These pressures sapped the strength of many white families. Alcoholism, divorce, and other destructive forces gnawed away at marital bonds. Historian Carol Bleser, in her pioneering work on Southern marriages during the Civil War, has shown the subtle and complex ways in which wartime might restructure relationships between marriage partners. The strains of Confederate surrender could and did cause irreparable damage for many Southerners. Edmund Ruffin, who had been one of the first to fire on Fort Sumter, took his own life in 1865 with a shotgun. Suicide was more common among men, but not exclusively a male prerogative. The *Charleston Daily Courier* reported a woman's suicide on February 6, 1867: "To accomplish her object, the poor deranged lady had first secured a rope around her neck, the end of which was attached to a spike in the side of the house, and sinking down upon her knees, the rope was thus drawn tight, which caused strangulation to ensue. Mrs. Range leaves several small children." Mental breakdowns were frequently reported. According to a Virginia woman, writing in 1873, "I heard the saddest thing the other day. My friend, Mrs. Newton, who lives near Dabney's ferry is deranged and has been sent to an asylum in Staunton. Her poor little girls have gone to their grandfather's to live. They say the care of her large estate, debt and other troubles were the cause." Newton's withdrawal to an asylum was but one road, including exile and suicide, that Southern women might take in their escape from reality.

Quite clearly, the cult of the Lost Cause captured the imagination of many Southern women in the wake of the war, with the vanquished planter class especially eager to right the wrongs of wartime. Lengthy literary campaigns were waged to that end (they will be explored in depth in the next chapter), but no more complex and contradictory problem faced former Confederates than their views on race. Many white women were intent on rewriting race relations and indulged in a remembrance of things imagined.

Henrietta Daingerfield described in her memoir of war the valor of an escaped black woman who sought shelter with her during wartime. "Our Amy was not a slave," she gushed, "but she was as loving and faithful as though she had been." Daingerfield's praise of Amy posits that slave status is somehow tied to faith and love—not involuntary servitude. This former mistress also claimed that a freedman, known as Uncle Levi, wanted to stay to work for her father *without* financial compensation. "Oh, no master, just please give me free papers, but you don't owe me anything," she relates him saying. "I owes you for a happy home, de care of my wife, and my little children, an a restin' place beside the wife of my youth, but marse, please I want to die a free man, tho' I have lived a happy slave." Another former slave owner reported that after she had offered an ex-slave freedom, clothing, and free passage to Liberia, her offer was spurned. "All felt very much mortified and hurt," she insisted, "that after this love for 'Mass Bush' and herself, and their years of faithful service to the fambly, she could think of sending them away from her, and especially to Africa, to live with wild 'niggers,' lions and tigers." These anecdotes concerning former servants fulfilled a number of fantasies for white tale-tellers, but they were only part of a campaign to re-create the past.

Approved and distributed by the United Daughters of the Confederacy, Matthew Page Andrews's book *Women of the South in War Times* (1920) included the following testimony from former mistress Loula Kendall Rogers: "We were never allowed . . . to speak of our colored dependents as 'slaves' but as 'house servants and field hands' and my father never failed to dismiss an overseer who was unkind to them." Rogers goes on to claim, "It was quite a heavy expense to furnish all of their clothing, shoes, blankets, hats, fuel and provisions, yet he not only did this, but being a physician provided needful medicines and careful attention in case of sickness."

Within romanticized portraits such as these, it is no wonder that former slaves are painted as docile and grateful: "The first greenbacks [notes issued by the U. S. government] were brought to one family by a former dining-room servant. His mistress, unable to pay him wages,

A Lady Bountiful image taken from *Dem Good Ole Times* (1906). Through literary propaganda, whites in the South reinforced the image of white benevolence and black dependence.

had advised him to seek employment elsewhere. At the end of a week, he returned, saying 'Mistiss, here is five dollahs. I'm making twenty dollahs a month and rations waitin' on one uh de Yankee officers. I'll bring you my wages evvy week."

These tales of "Negro fealty" stand side by side with vicious attacks on black disloyalty. One woman argued that before the war, "the fear of a negro could not cross the brains of a white man or woman of the South. It is only years since the war that atrocities have been committed by negroes in the South that have made our blood curdle and men to tell their wives to keep a pistol near them. . . . Their minds have been poisoned; they don't trust us and we don't trust them. With the exception of a few of the old ones now fast dying out, there is not a bit of old feeling left."

Lost Cause advocates further complained that blacks suffered from their freedom as well. Myrta Lockett Avary claimed, "After freedom, they [blacks] began to die of pulmonary complaints. There were frequent epidemics of typhoid fever, quarters not being well kept. 'The race is dying out,' said prophets. Negroes began to grow mad. An insane negro was rarely heard of during slavery. Regular hours, regular work, chiefly out of doors, sobriety, freedom from care and responsibility had kept the negro singularly exempt from insanity and various other afflictions that curse the white. Big lunatic asylums established for negroes soon after the war and their continual enlargement tell their own story." This bigoted author capped off her analysis with observations on child abuse and syphilis, which she claimed ran rampant within the black community as well.

Reconstruction politics were at the root of many of these tirades and debates. Former slave owner were enraged that they were forced to court black votes, and many simply ignored the realities of black suffrage—a right that diminished after Reconstruction when conservative

---

ABOVE: "AUNT DORCAS," A ROMANTICIZED IMAGE OF MAMMY AND CHILD.

old-time Southerners, known as Bourbon Democrats, returned to power, and black electoral participation dramatically declined. But during the immediate postwar years Union occupation imposed Republican rule and "Negro politics" was a bitter pill for ex-Confederates to swallow.

Virginian Sarah Rice Pryor whined, "Ignorant negroes, or tools of corrupt men, were elected to fill important offices; or were defeated by methods which could not but

Kitty, Slave Girl Who Refused Freedom, Brought Division of Methodist Church in 1844

Kitty's Home - Covington, Ga. - 1916.

be degrading to the despairing white minority." Pryor was infuriated by the way in which African Americans pursued their own political agenda, believing as she did that they should vote the interest of their employers only. A South Carolina white woman wrote in 1888: "But we had to work hard with the darkies to convince them that the Democrats would not vote them back into slavery. . . . You would have laughed had you seen the front verandah filled with darkies & father speaking to them (day before election). . . . He got most of our tenant to vote right or if not to stay at home & not vote at all. John Anderson was the only one to vote with the Rads! (good for nothing thing) He will not be on the place next year." Planters used their power to cajole or threaten their workers, trying to buy or bully votes.

The rising tide of Lost Cause nationalism posed a considerable threat to Southern blacks in the postwar era. As early as 1866 planters sponsored "tournaments" at which war veterans might perform, wearing full Confederate regalia topped by plumed hats—despite Yankee bans on the wearing of Confederate uniforms. But this "dress-up" game cannot conceal the real drama that unfolded during this period as the white South confronted the reality of millions of previously enslaved African Americans emerging as Southern citizens, defiant and unwilling to return to the good old days.

ABOVE: A CLIPPING FROM A UNITED DAUGHTERS OF THE CONFEDERACY SCRAPBOOK
CAPTURES THE SENSATIONALIST, SUGAR-COATED VIEW OF RACE RELATIONS PROMOTED
BY WHITE APOLOGISTS FOR SLAVERY.

ELECTIONEERING AT THE SOUTH.—SKETCHED BY W. L. SHEPPARD.—[SEE PAGE 601.]

ABOVE: A NORTHERN VIEW OF RECONSTRUCTION POLITICS.

The ideological standoff during Reconstruction included sexual as well as political dimensions. Terrain was contested from the kitchen to the courtroom, from the street corner to the statehouse. African Americans had sprawling agendas in the wake of emancipation, but clearly the integrity of the family and the protection of black women was of utmost concern within their community. Laws may have changed, but exploitative habits died hard. When the basic rights of citizenship were extended to blacks through Constitutional amendments, ex-Confederates attempted extralegal means to perpetuate racial injustice.

Black leader Reverend Henry McNeal Turner observed: "Southern fanatics rode that hobby everywhere, 'That if you free the negro he will want to marry our daughters and sister,' that was another foolish dream. What do we want with their daughters and sisters? We have as much beauty as they. Look at our ladies, do you want more beauty than that? *All we ask of the white man is to let our ladies alone,* and they need not fear us." But fear preyed on the minds of white Southerners, and the theme of miscegenation (a phrase coined by politicians in 1864) created political hysteria. An 1866 editorial in a black paper in Augusta, Georgia, thundered: "No wonder then, that the cry is loud and long when there is a prospect through the agency of a new born freedom, of a man with a *dark skin* leading to the altar a woman with a *white skin.* But is the cry reasonable? We think not." The great intellectual W.E.B. DuBois, writing in 1921, was particularly outraged by the charade of Southern chivalry. "Many a man and woman in the South have lived in wedlock as holy as Adam and Eve and brought forth their born and golden children," he said. "But because the darker woman was helpless her chivalrous and whiter mate could cast her off at his pleasure and publicly sneer at the body he had privately blasphemed."

Sexual hypocrisy, so long a fashion among the planter class, which condemned "amalgamation" while engaging in sexual relations with blacks, was finally openly attacked by angry freed people. "Let any man turn his eyes and view the faces of three-fourths of the colored race and what does he see reflected there?" demanded DuBois. *"The shadow of some white father. . . .* Who is to blame for this boundary line being broken? Is it the colored man? Certainly not; for many a time it was more than his life was worth to attempt to resist the *dishonor* of his own flesh and blood. Was the colored woman to blame? By no means, for she could not help herself."

These attacks upon "white superiors" turned Lost Cause advocates wild, and even women joined in the campaign. One of the most pointed of revisionists, Myrta Lockett Avary, made bold and sweeping arguments in her political volume *Dixie After the War* (1906). She like others of her intellectual circle manifested extreme anxiety over the questions of flesh, blood, and interracial sex that raged during this tumultuous period, as they had for generations. White Southerners were discomforted when these kinds of issues were explored in the public spotlight—rather than behind closed doors, where the South wished to continue with its taboo tradition.

ABOVE: A CURRIER AND IVES PRINT TITLED *A COLORED BEAUTY.*

Nevertheless Lost Cause writers rallied with sensationalist tomes—many of which were billed as histories. Some of this work featured innocent white heroines and brute savage freedmen. According to one publication: "A squad of blacks marched, bound the owner, a prominent aged citizen, pillaged his house, and then before his eyes bound his maiden daughter and proceeded to fight among themselves for her possession." In this particular version the daughter stabs a freedman through the heart before being beaten to death, while "negroes talked openly of killing our white men and taking white women for wives." White supremacists closed ranks against these alleged threats, fueling tensions and advocating vigilante violence.

Patterns of violence described by the white community were challenged by the black press. As one Georgia newspaper reported in 1866, "We are informed that a most fiendish outrage was committed near Hamburg, South Carolina one night last week by five *white* men, disguised with masks. They went to the house of Chandler Garrot, a *colored* man, and each violated the person of his wife, a *colored* woman. . . . Comment upon the conduct of these men is unnecessary. Why do not our city dailies mention some of the outrages committed daily and nightly by white men against the freedmen? If a freedman commits an offense against a *white* it is immediately heralded, but when the freedmen suffer, the world seldom hears of it."

Embattled race relations took a tremendous toll on blacks, who, like many Southern whites, were trying to "keep pauperism at bay." Many African American families in the South were headed by females, whose job prospects were limited. As one observer reported from King William County, Virginia, "there is little call for female help, and women with children are not desired." Conditions for the employed were harsh as well. In August 1867 Angaline Robbins, a black widow supporting three small children in Greensboro, Georgia, appealed to her local branch of the Bureau of Refugees, Freedmen and Abandoned Lands (the Freedman's Bureau) to intercede with her employer. She had been working in Gordon Ascue's cotton and corn fields, but when it came time to be paid, as was all too often the custom, she was driven off the land. After freedwoman Cornelia Whitley complained about her employer to the bureau in September 1865, she was beaten by his wife for going to the agency for help.

A federal officer wrote to his commander in December 1865 from Magnolia, Mississippi, describing conditions African Americans endured: "It is my earnest conviction that they are the most persecuted

and the most patient people in the world. A bare record of the cruelties
perpetrated by their late masters towards them in this vicinity would
make your blood run cold. Whipping, shooting and hanging are three
furies that follow in the footsteps of the black man's freedom." The officer
also charged that Freedman's Bureau trials were farces, with local whites
often willing to go so far as to "remove cause of complaint"—i.e., to
murder any African American willing to testify against them.

In face of mounting social chaos and interracial violence, a handful
of white women publicly supported efforts to restore order but via
white supremacy. These token women were allowed outside their
appointed spheres and into the public realm in order to champion their
sex, but only within the prescribed formulas established by white men.
Particularly clever women were able to twist this liability to their advantage upon occasion. Some white Southern suffrage leaders such as
Belle Kearney of Mississippi and Kate Gordon of Louisiana became
race baiters, hoping to tap into white solidarity to overcome male chau-
vinism by proposing that women (i.e., white women) be given suffrage as
a means of countering the black vote. Dynamic Georgia suffragist
Rebecca Latimer Felton, the first woman to become a U.S. senator, also
manipulated issues to her own advantage. In an 1897 speech on Tybee
Island, Georgia, she exhorted, "If it needs lynching to protect woman's
dearest possession . . . I say 'lynch' a thousand times a week if necessary."
By the time Felton offered her solution, white vigilantes had resorted to

a reign of terror that resulted in a lynching in America on the average of once every two days. The 1890s were a decade of blood and terror.

Lynching and race riots undermined the Lost Cause campaign to restore luster to the fallen South. Thousands of women all across the region had worked for more than a generation to redeem their fallen nation through memorial associations and Confederate women's groups. In 1894 many of these organizations banded together to form the United Daughters of the Confederacy (UDC), which became a powerful force in the South during the first half of the twentieth century.

By the close of the nineteenth century, Confederate veterans' associations were shrinking but the UDC managed to continue growing

LYNCHING VICTIMS WERE TOO FAMILIAR AN IMAGE IN THE SOUTHERN LANDSCAPE AT THE END OF THE NINETEENTH CENTURY. HOWEVER, SUCH PHOTOGRAPHS RARELY APPEARED IN NEWSPAPERS OF THE DAY.

from only seventeen thousand members in 1900 to near seventy thousand by 1920. The organization mounted a clever campaign of inclusion, offering the Southern Cross of Honor to any veteran, his widow, or his descendant. Hundreds of thousands could lay claim to the Confederate dream: "Fate denied victory, but has crowned [us] with glorious immortality." These indefatigable fund-raisers not only established Confederate memorial days and cemetery celebrations but they single-mindedly campaigned to build monumental memorials and dot the nation with markers to preserve Confederate values and memories. UDC members also determined "to collect and preserve materials for a truthful history of the war . . . [and] to endeavor to have used in Southern schools only such histories as are just and true."

This educational component comprised a brilliant strategy, with the UDC offering cash prizes for essay contests that they sponsored at both private and public schools. They also offered school libraries subscriptions to the *Confederate Veteran* and donated UDC sponsored volumes such as Andrews's *Women of the South in War Times.* Their campaigns for politically correct language were pioneering, as they argued in annual reports that every UDC member must challenge the misleading use of the term "Civil War" and correct it with the preferred "War Between the States." (Over the century following Confederate surrender there was a progressive evolution in the South of the acceptable term—from the "War of Northern Aggression" to the "War for Southern Independence" to, finally, the "War Between the States.")

Children of the Confederacy, a junior wing of the UDC, offered white Southerners an opportunity to affiliate themselves with the Lost Cause almost from infancy. Catechism included enlightenment on such important issues as the "true cause of the war," which was described as "disregard, on the part of the States of the North, for the rights of the Southern or slaveholding states." Junior historians might lead groups in discussions ranging from "Negro Folk Tales" to "Heroes of the Confederate Navy."

Lucrative scholarships for both male and female descendants of veterans were funded by the UDC, with the College of William and Mary, in Williamsburg, Virginia, and other institutions welcoming these donations. The UDC also actively sought to engage members in activist campaigns, such as annual petitions to state legislatures to abolish the Lincoln's birthday holiday. Fund drives, meetings, annual conventions, and costume cotillions occupied many an adult member through a lifetime. And at the end of that life, the family of a deceased

MILDRED LEWIS RUTHERFORD, LONGTIME PRESIDENT OF GEORGIA'S UNITED
DAUGHTERS OF THE CONFEDERACY, AND A STAUNCH LEADER OF THE
NATIONAL ORGANIZATION.

member was supplied with a small silk flag of the Confederacy to
accompany the departed in their caskets. The UDC provided community for its membership family from the cradle to the grave.

Although many UDC members were actively involved in social
welfare within their churches and communities, they were not in the
forefront of social reform. Yet while women's suffrage was a campaign
that most UDC members disdained, UDC leadership in Richmond and

statewide supported bids for women's admission to the University of Virginia during a 1913 movement for state-sponsored coeducation. Likewise, UDC members gloried in women's abilities to surpass men's efforts, particularly their own coup in establishing the Jefferson Davis Memorial. After trying for three years but soliciting less than 10 percent of their budget, in 1899 the United States Confederate Veterans turned over the memorial project to the UDC in hopes that they could rescue this flagging drive to honor the Confederate president in the former Confederate capital. The women modified the overly ambitious plans, set a reasonable goal, raised seventy thousand dollars, and by 1906 broke ground. At the dedication ceremony in 1907 the governor of Virginia, Claude Swanson, lauded their efforts. "This magnificent memorial is a gift from the United Daughters of the Confederacy," he exulted, "whose loyalty to the Confederate cause is ardent and lasting, and whose splendid qualities and patriotism was sufficient to stimulate and made great and glorious many people." More than 200,000 spectators gathered to hear this praise, while a thousand former veterans paraded to celebrate the unveiling.

During the past century the UDC has cataloged an impressive record. Confederate monuments stand in twenty-seven states as well as

CHILDREN WERE INDUCTED AS ACOLYTES INTO THE UNITED DAUGHTERS OF THE CONFEDERACY.

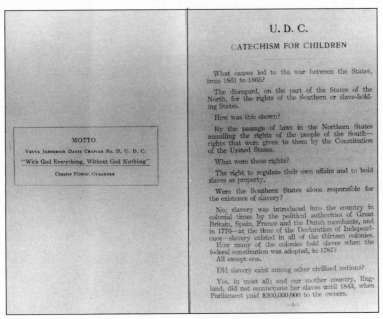

CONFEDERACY QUILT MADE BY FIRST LADY VARINA DAVIS.

the District of Columbia, Virginia ranking at the top with 223 memorials and Georgia a distant second with 145. But Confederate tributes are also as far flung as the Jefferson Davis Memorial Highway in San Diego, California, a lone tablet marker in Washington State, and another marker in Montana. By 1982 there were 1,120 Confederate memorials, and while not all of them were funded and dedicated by UDC chapters, the majority owe their origins if not their completion to those tireless crusaders.

The United Daughters of the Confederacy is not a dying movement; indeed, chapters flourish throughout the South, and since 1965 the group has coordinated a "Massing of the Flag" ceremony in Richmond on June 3 (Jefferson Davis's birthday). During this annual event participants pledge: "I salute the Confederate flag, with affection, reverence and undying remembrance." This campaign of "undying remembrance" is Confederate women's most effective legacy. Their efforts to rewrite the history of their failed nation have been amazing, and while the stain of surrender can never be erased, generations of Southern ladies embody the stubborn refusal of plantation values to die a quiet death.

Indeed, the "pilgrimage weeks" sponsored by local historical and preservation societies, in which plantations recreate the Old South with costumes and other trappings, in many ways embalm a departed South that perhaps never lived outside Confederate imaginations. After the Civil War wiped out the hopes and dreams of many aspiring to plantation gentility, the cult of the Lost Cause welcomed all to the well of fond remembrance. And as white Southerners drank deeply from this fountain, they revived and toasted the plantation legend. In its contemporary incarnation, this legend, this body of fact and fiction, remains one of the most potent symbols of Southern culture, an icon that has left an indelible imprint on Southern history.

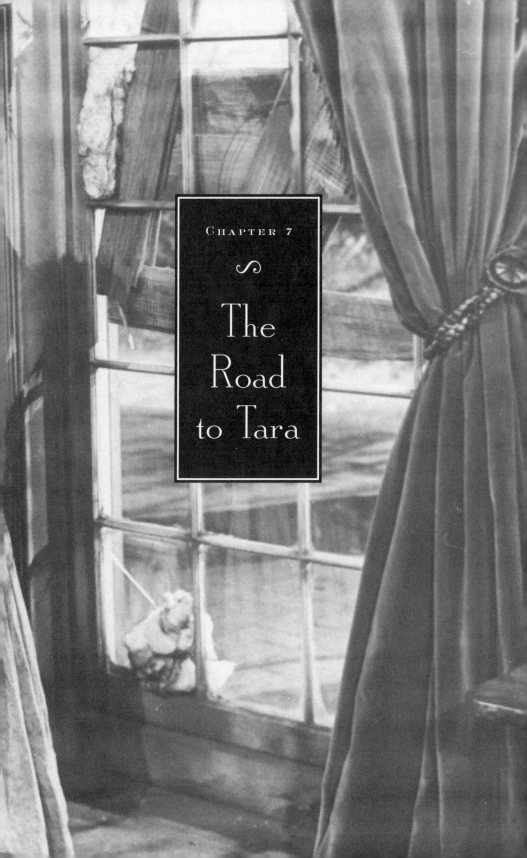

CHAPTER 7

The
Road
to Tara

The Road
to Tara

A long road leads from the heroic memorialization launched by the generation of defeated Confederates to the elevation of Tara as the symbol of the Old South. By embellishing pomp and spectacle, by celebrating with pageant and elaborate statuary, by rewriting with reckless abandon, the vanquished South rose again to a splendor that far outshone foundation in reality. In "Dixie," the song most closely associated with Confederate nationalism, the lyrics remind us, "old times there are not forgotten." Legends are crucial links for the chain of memory that binds the vanquished past to the glorious future.

But the cloth of legend is not woven wholly from fantasy. Legends reveal our selective retelling of the past, how we document the facts and then embroider with telling if inaccurate detail. Like gossip, legends let us know as much about the storyteller as they do about events. The durability of plantation sagas tells us about our present as well as our past.

The opening pages of Oliver Taylor Cardwell's *Life on a Plantation* ring familiar: "This is the story of life on a plantation located in the heart of Virginia, a place called Wildway. . . . I was born at Wildway, the youngest of eleven children. My father owned the six hundred acre plantation on which tobacco and other farm crops were grown. We lived in a big rambling house of thirteen rooms, an attic, a cellar and three porches. . . . Music was in the air all over the plantation. . . . Aunt

---

PAGES 188–89: SCARLETT (VIVIEN LEIGH) AND MAMMY (HATTIE McDANIELS)
CONFRONTING REALITY DURING RECONSTRUCTION.
OPPOSITE: THIS IMAGE OF A PLANTER COUPLE AND SLAVES, FROM *DEM GOOD
OLE TIMES* (1906), TYPIFIES THE STYLIZED SOUTHERN NOSTALGIA CREATED
FOR THE MASS MARKET.

Hayes Plantation in Edenton, North Carolina, built around 1801.

Frances was our mammy. She helped my mother with the eleven children." This is a classic image from the genteel antebellum South, but discovering that it was published the same year that Americans orbited the moon and Martin Luther King was assassinated—1968—demonstrates the persistence of this genre.

Scholars argue that the plantation legend in novel form developed during the antebellum era—beginning with the work of John Esten Cooke, John Pendelton Kennedy, and William Gilmore Simms. Whatever its origins, the popularity of this legendary literature certainly predates the Civil War. During the war the legends of Southern life continued to exert a strong hold on many Americans. That mythical repository, the fictional plantation, could spellbind even the most loyal of Yankees. While Union and Confederate soldiers squared off to do battle, *Harper's Weekly* (one of the most popular periodicals in the North during the war years, notable for its vivid illustrations of battle and camp life) carried an advertisement for *Maum Guinea and her Plantation Children,* a lavishly illustrated "romance" novel. The author, a Mrs. Victor, was described as capturing the "power, pathos and humor" of Christmas week among Louisiana slaves. Her Philadelphia publisher promised this work would remind its reader of Uncle Tom, and indeed Maum

Guinea, like many works before and many more to follow, cashed in on some of the same romanticizations. The formula required the trappings of the plantation—lush exotic exteriors with tortured interiors—blacks and whites colorized by treacly sentiment.

The power of these settings and characters and the intense response such combinations evoked were established in earnest by the end of the Civil War. The great work of glorification and memorialization begun by Confederate veterans and their adolescent acolytes spread northward through an effective literary campaign. Many Southern writers actively sought this creative outlet as a way to return to a past that never was.

In a good number of the partisan volumes that came out during these years, Southern women are not simply pivotal to the plot, but come to symbolize the South itself. In John William De Forest's *Bloody Chasm* (1881), the heroine, "Virginia," is forced to fend for herself, her mammy, her aunt, and a young black freedwoman. De Forest's body of postwar work and the later novels of Cary Eggleston demonstrate the way in which authors recast Southern history by showing the South in a feminine light, as a woman victimized by suffering. These fictions nearly always celebrated a theme of reconciliation, one that featured woman's submission—a hand in marriage.

Northern authors might share in this literary revisionism, but nearly all Southern writers were required to adopt this lockstep plot. Southern author Sherwood Bonner abandoned her hometown of Holly Springs, Mississippi (and her husband and child along the way), for northern literary circles in the 1880s. Settled in Boston, she discovered that audiences craved the exotic flavor of the plantation South and

---

ABOVE: TURN-OF-THE-CENTURY POSTCARD ILLUSTRATING THE POPULARIZATION OF RACIST SENSIBILITY.

expected her, as a Southern writer, to deliver familiar if not stereotyped depictions of languid whites and exotic blacks. Until Ellen Glasgow and William Faulkner, Southern writers were trapped in clichés, churning out variants of simple stereotypes. Even if these Southern stylists did not write in the style of *Uncle Tom's Cabin*, their characters rarely moved beyond the vernacular, with the exception of a handful of black writers and the incomparable Kate Chopin. But Chopin's short stories and her masterpiece, *The Awakening*, were long buried under the label of local color.

The romantic gush of this prose astonishes the postmodern reader, as exemplified by a poem found on the dedication page of *Shadowland: Stories of the South* (1906):

> *Beyond the purple hazy trees,*
> *Of summers utmost boundaries,*
> *Beyond the sands, beyond the seas,*
> *Beyond the range of eyes like these*
> *And only in the reach of the*
> *Enraptured gaze of memory*
> *There lies a land long lost to me—*
> *The land of Used to be—*

And so the vanquished South wrote its way out of defeat. There were notable failings, nevertheless, most especially in the category of school texts. After Lee surrendered at Appomattox, the Pilgrims replaced Jamestown as the "lead story" in historical textbooks. The march of economic success and capitalist expansion required Calvinist origins, and Yankee typewriters triumphed over quaint Southern quills.

Yet the Southern quill could not be still. What Southern writer, white or black, does not attribute his or her talents and interests to storytelling within the family? From the front porch to the airwaves, the Southern accent provides confessional intrigue. So children steeped in memories laced with self-pity and grand illusion hear that cultural hum, a hint of melody just below the surface.

Southern education has always had an evangelical twang. Southern juvenile literature took aim at Yankee falsehoods in such works as Sallie Southall Cotten's *Negro Folk Lore Stories* (1923), subtitled *What Aunt Dorcas told Little Elsie*. The book opens: "Elsie Gilmore was born in New England and knew all about Plymouth Rock and the Pilgrim Fathers. She could tell about the Battle of Bunker Hill and describe

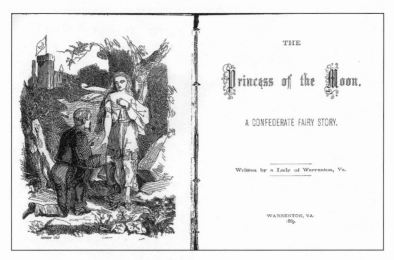

OPENING PAGES OF A CONFEDERATE FAIRY TALE.

Paul Revere's Raid, but she knew absolutely nothing about Southern negroes. So when her mother went to visit a school friend in Alabama and took Elsie with her, the little girl was fascinated by the shining black faces and strange dialect of the negro women. . . ." Little Elsie is treated to tales from Aunt Dorcas that emphasize the warmth and familial relations between black and white.

In the era before comic books, fairy tales displayed Confederate superheroes, among them Mrs. Semmes Ives's *The Princess of the Moon,* a work privately published in Warrenton, Virginia, in 1869. Ives addressed her words, "especially to you, little sufferers of the South, who during the war waged against us endured hunger and cold; were made homeless and fatherless." The tale begins, "It was after the dreadful struggle between North and South that a poor Confederate soldier wandered in a wood near the ruins of his once splendid home. . . ." The wandering soldier ends up on the moon and falls in love with a princess. He is visited by Yankees who are surrounded by dragons at the wave of his good fairy's wand. Finally he is reunited with a faithful servant and—no surprise to any of us—wins the princess to be his own.

Most children's literature was manufactured for domestic Southern consumption and necessarily had a local audience. By contrast many travel accounts and memoirs—even those that might appear to be targeted at a Southern readership—were not only sold to Northern publishers but found London publishers as well. The post–Civil War resurgence of interest in Southern plantations was launched by the

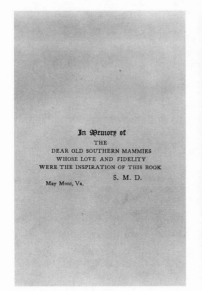

Title and dedication pages of a nostalgic memoir — an example of a
"remembrance of things imagined." Lavish treatment of the mammy is
a staple of this genre.

"Great South" series, which appeared in *Scribner's* in 1873–1874. This extensive project, covering 450 pages and including 430 engravings, made a name for its author, Edward King, who is credited with the "discovery" of George Washington Cable. *Scribner's* continued to mine this vein of Southern literature, in 1881 beginning the publication of Joel Chandler Harris's Uncle Remus tales and shortly thereafter adding Thomas Nelson Page's Marse Chan stories. Although these authors penned fiction, their portraits varied only slightly in theme and tone from the "nonfiction" that appeared alongside, such as "Uncle Tom Without a Cabin." The editors of *The Century* published an article in July 1885 on the Ku Klux Klan, appended by an editorial comment that was near endorsement, arguing that "a growing sympathy with the whites of the South will draw interest to this account of the Klan." Southern literature and Northern journalism began to converge into a single ideological flow of racist invective.

Northern audiences were softened by decades of Southern tales of white suffering. From the period 1865–1885, most Southern authors focused on the idealization of the antebellum period and the dark age enforced by Confederate surrender. From E. A. Pollard's *The Lost Cause* (1866) on through to apologists in the twentieth century, a steady stream of romantic, sentimentalized portrayals appeared. Some harp on Confederate parallels with the Lost Cause of Scotland—the Jacobite movement for Scottish independence crushed by the British in 1745. Others glorify the rural, pre-industrial nature of the Old South. But in both versions there are fundamental distortions of the interplay between black and white, gender and class, capitalism and paternalism, within the complex skein of southern social relations.

An explosion of interest in Southern plantation lore began in the late 1890s and has continued into the current century. Once Southern and Northern men went to war on the same side—in the brief but "splendid little war" with Spain between April and August in 1898—the full cycle of military reconciliation was completed. The Spanish-American War launched the South's spiritual restoration, and periodical publishers and booksellers alike responded to this reconciliation.

The primary genre of this period was the plantation diary, journal, or memoir written by whites about their own experiences. Many of these used the Civil War as the focal event. Certainly most exemplary within this category is Mary Boykin Chesnut's *Diary From Dixie,* which was first published in 1906 and edited by Isabella Martin and Myrta Lockett Avary. Avary herself would publish her own historical reconstruction that same year: *Dixie After the War: An Exposition of Social Conditions Existing in the South During the Twelve Years Succeeding the Fall of Richmond.* Her colorful and opinionated volume retold the familiar narratives of Confederate suffering. For example, she recounts the tale of a woman whose reduced circumstances force her to take money from a former slave who has secured employment with a Yankee officer. When the white woman tries to refuse his generosity—in this fable—he replies, "You take care uh me all my life, Mistiss an' learnt me how to work. I orter do what I kin fuh you." This sentiment contrasts starkly with reminiscences of the war from WPA interviews; one

A songsheet depicting the breadth and depth of racist caricature. Entertainment, advertising, art, and cultural artifact reflecting the degradation of African Americans masqueraded as "Southern nostalgia."

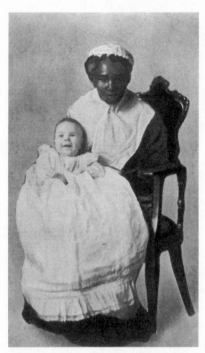

Mississippi slave recalled: "When de war wus ober, Old Marse called all de slaves . . . an' tole dem dat dey wus freed, an' sed iffen dey wud stay wid him an' wurk he wud pay dem fur deir wurk . . . old Marse paid dem at de end uf de year lak he sed he wud. But de next year most uf dem wint ter nudder place ter wurk."

These Confederate revisionist texts are full of arrogance. Eliza Ripley claims in her memoirs of antebellum Louisiana: "I am no apologist for slavery: the whites suffered more from its demoralizing influence than the blacks, but we were born to it, grew up with it, lived with it, and it was our daily life. We did well by it; no people could have done better. It is past now. When I tell of my own home, it is to tell of the plantation homes of everybody I knew. We did not differ or vary to any extent in our modes of life and management." White denial and racial superiority overflow in this literature.

Southerners were certainly concerned with glorifying the past—but they also wished to demonstrate a tradition of harmony that they hoped could characterize black-white relations in the post-war South. Margaret Mitchell, growing up in Atlanta during the city's worst race riot, in 1906, remembered with terror when she was just five, "they fought all day just a block behind our house." She and other authors of plantation epics chose not even to hint at these aspects of Southern race relations, relying on a culture of dissemblance and denial.

This literature of dissemblance blossomed in the final decade of the nineteenth century, when a black majority and white minority began to crusade against the inhumanity of lynching. By 1894 a lynching was reported on an average of once every two days in the South. During this same period, black crusader Ida B. Wells-Barnett demonstrated that

---

ABOVE: "OUR MAMMY." THIS PHOTOGRAPHIC "EVIDENCE" WAS INTRODUCED FREQUENTLY IN MEMOIRS TO AUTHENTICATE TALES OF RACIAL HARMONY.

AN ELDERLY BLACK WOMAN (UNIDENTIFIED, PRESUMABLY A FORMER MAMMY) POSING WITH VIRGINIA BRIDE ELIZABETH HUNTLEY. THESE PORTRAITS WERE INTENDED TO VALIDATE WARM RELATIONS BETWEEN BLACKS AND WHITES.

the facts of most cases did not entail even a hint of the alleged cause of lynchings, the rape of a white woman by a black man. Indeed, Wells-Barnett chronicled white-on-black atrocities in her lectures and pamphlets, informing readers, for instance, of the murder of a pregnant black woman and detailing her death in gripping detail. During her international crusade against "Southern horrors," her speeches on lynching held her listeners spellbound. By lambasting these atrocities and by testifying against what she called this "red record," Wells-Barnett electrified her audience. With this kind of bad press, white Southerners redoubled their efforts to create racially harmonious folklore, and legends poured forth.

A second, extremely popular trend in plantation literature involved letters or stories composed for offspring or descendants. This technique allowed the author to "explain" the past to an unquestioning listener to whom the Civil War was not even a memory but an event imagined in precise detail. A woman composing a memoir for her granddaughter recalled: "In one of my rare visits South to my own people, the old time darkies, our former slaves, walked twenty miles to see 'Miss Nancy' and her little daughter, and the latter, your dear mother, would often be surprised when taken impulsively in their big black arms, and hugged and kissed and cried over for ol' times' sakes' . . ." This woman proclaimed without a smidgen of doubt: "I want you to know that the Southerner understands to this day, the negro's character better than the Northerner, and is in the main kinder to, and more forbearing with him."

This propagandistic writing, much of which included photographs to authenticate the stories, was intended to redeem the relationship between former owners and ex-slaves, one being tarnished by "ignorant" and "malicious" fabricators. Rarely is the romanticized figure of the Mammy omitted. The following introduction is typical: "'Good morning, Aunt Susan. I have brought you some coffee and sugar, and some tobacco for your pipe,' said Virginia at the old woman's cabin door next morning. 'Old Aunt Susan,' as everybody on the place called the blind woman who alone remained of the seven hundred slaves who had once worked and sung and danced at Frescati, looked very comfortable and well cared for, as she sat in her deep rocking-chair in the sunshine that streamed in at the cabin door." We discover almost immediately that this mammy has been abandoned by her blood family and that Colonel Prescott, of her "white family," pays one of her granddaughters to care for her.

Whites cherished the notion that blacks could not take care of themselves. ". . . Yes, Dorothy dear, a lot of children unprepared to enjoy the Emancipation Proclamation were suddenly confronted with life's problems," penned one writer, who claimed to be collecting black folk takes. In one particularly fanciful volume, another author tells the story of a young black boy who is caught in the clutches of both an evil black stepmother (abandoned by his black father) and the Freedman's

Bureau. The young boy seeks a white neighbor's protection, looking to the son of a Confederate hero for help. In response the boy's legal guardian and stepmother seek vengeance through the press. The headlines screech: "KIDNAPPER! Decoyed a delicate, ten-year old boy from his mother's side and refuses to give him up! Wants to revive the days of slavery, no doubt, but will see that no such violation of the law will be permitted. Freedman's Bureau will attend to it! Case called at ten o'clock at Court House to-morrow!"

The trial is worthy of an afternoon television drama, a sensationalized "Freedpeople's Court" that has the young boy pleading to stay with his white benefactor and not return to his wicked black stepmother. The Freedman's Bureau agent is a man called Mr. Garrison—a name most closely associated with radical abolitionism in the North and misguided Yankee philanthropy in the South. But this Garrison is transfixed by the vision of the young boy begging for mercy. Acted out in the sectional melodrama of these fables, Garrison's view of Southern paternalism is magically transformed and the black boy is rescued from the "wicked and incompetent" black family and delivered into a white household.

This celebration of familial interracial relations was intended as both a soothing exercise in propaganda and a means to exorcise the agonies of slavery. Whites bemoaned the loss of their beloved servants, particularly their mammies: "Poor little children nowadays," wrote one, "who change their nurses continually can never know or understand the deep lasting love which existed between Southern children and their mammies." Other passages reveal a maudlin sense of mutual dependence and spiritual affinity: "the blind woman's quick ear caught a muffled sound of sobbing, and holding out her arms she took Virginia to their shelter, quieting her with such tender crooning as only negro nurses know."

BOOK COVER FROM *AUNT JEMIMY'S MAXIMS* (1909), AN EXAMPLE OF A WHITE AUTHOR WRITING IN "BLACKFACE."

These memoirs, which purported to retell the good old days, are surpassed by an even more creative genre: the African-American memoir written by a white. This phenomenon antedated the Civil War: *Autobiography of a Female Slave* was published by "Mattie Griffiths" (1857), whose "authentic" narrative was in reality a piece of anti-slavery fiction composed by the white daughter of a Kentucky slave holder. Dialect tales also became increasingly popular during the postbellum period. Sherwood Bonner steadily supplied the Northern magazine market and Kate Chopin earned an income including patois and colorful Creole backgrounds in her fictional sketches of Louisiana life. Quite naturally, other Southern writers followed suit. The wife of Confederate hero General George Pickett, LaSalle Corbell Pickett, wrote a series of books, published beginning in 1900, that capitalized on the craze for "Negro folklore," including *Kunnoo Sperits and Others, Yule Log* (which included the story "Wuz Santa Claus a Nigger dat Year"), *Ebil Eye,* and *Jinny.*

In Pickett's and other such works, white voices enter the text only to frame the "verbatim" black chronicles, published wholly in dialect. As linguists have reminded us, this "black English" is really white racist rendering of African-American language. "Wuz" for "was" and "dere" for "there" were not the spellings used by blacks; rather, the way in which whites consistently misspelled black speech conveyed a sense of racial superiority. Whites' perfect grammar and spelling are the bookends that enclose these "black voices" and are meant to provide stark contrast.

The content of these white prefaces and epilogues as well as their style are designed to entrance Confederate descendants. Ruby Vaughn Bigger's volume, entitled *My Miss Nancy* (1924), begins, "Some of the happiest days of my childhood were spent at my grandfather's estate in Hanover County, surrounded by his loyal family servants—all Southern negroes, to whom I was affectionately known as 'little Mistis.'" And the dedication page gushes, "To you, whose happiest hours have been spent in the shelter of *your* Mammy's arms, surrounded by her tender care, I dedicate this little story."

Bigger's book begins with the ever-essential promise: "This is a true story." She then goes on to chronicle her search for a black woman called Mammy Veenie, who had raised Lady Astor, born into a prominent Virginia family, the Langhornes. Riding out to search in the woods near Greenwood, Virginia, the narrator admits her fear that "there was no more old Virginia. Mammies and Colonels and old romantic figures which have dwelt in the minds of every Southerner, I knew lived in

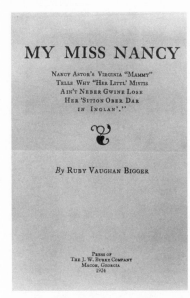

MY MISS NANCY

NANCY ASTOR'S VIRGINIA "MAMMY"
TELLS WHY "HER LITTL' MISTIS
AIN'T NEBER GWINE LOSE
HER 'SITION OBER DAR
IN INGLAN'."

By RUBY VAUGHAN BIGGER

PRESS OF
THE J. W. BURKE COMPANY
MACON, GEORGIA
1924

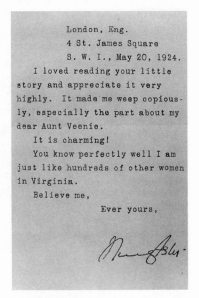

London, Eng.
4 St. James Square
S. W. I., May 20, 1924.
I loved reading your little
story and appreciate it very
highly. It made me weep copious-
ly, especially the part about my
dear Aunt Veenie.
It is charming!
You know perfectly well I am
just like hundreds of other women
in Virginia.
Believe me,
Ever yours,

WHITES OFTEN INSERTED TESTIMONIALS INTO VOLUMES TO "AUTHENTICATE" STORIES.
THESE FORMULAIC TALES EXAGGERATED AND ROMANTICIZED HARMONY BETWEEN THE
RACES IN THE PRE-WAR AND POST-WAR SOUTH. THIS PARTICULAR VOLUME
CELEBRATED NANCY ASTOR'S MAMMY.

imagination only. . . ." She almost gives up, then stumbles upon a cabin where, "lo and behold," the elderly black woman resides. Mammy Veenie then launches into thirty pages of dialogue recounting the good old days, before the white scribe brings this phantasmagorical tale to a close. "I turned from this little scene of a day forever gone, with a big lump in my throat," she writes, "longing for the olden days of happy childhood and the ever faithful Virginia Mammy."

Because of the highly charged nature of regional and racial attitudes, academics have avoided some of the more interesting aspects of this kind of material. Racist memorabilia is now widely collected, and indeed some of the largest collections have been established by African Americans: postcards, ceramics, cartoons, advertisements, and other artifacts display this vicious streak in popular culture. These vivid stereotypes demean blacks while allegedly enhancing whites.

The antiquated white literary tradition of a rose-colored plantation life embarrasses contemporary Southern liberals and rarely attracts serious study. Unlike racist memorabilia, which has been put under the spotlight to illuminate significant aspects of our past, these white literary products seem to have fallen between the cracks. Not rating as collectibles, in a sense they have become "dismissables." In some ways this

Lady Astor, the former Nancy Langhorne, in a reception line during
a visit to her former Virginia home, Mirador.

forbidden and shameful quality renders it "Confederate porn," something we know exists but would rather not allow for public consumption. Dragged out furtively and in private, it produces responses that
range from delight to revulsion. Without confrontation or exploration,
these images and attitudes proliferate unimpeded.

The literary images described above are far from harmless scrib-
blings—indeed they serve to demonize African Americans. During the
early part of the century they helped legitimize the Ku Klux Klan in
the North. After Thomas Dixon published *The Leopard's Spots* (1902),
followed by *The Clansmen* (1905) and *The Sins of the Father* (1912), his
Klan trilogy was translated to the screen by D. W. Griffith. His 1915
film, *Birth of a Nation,* was heralded as a brilliant masterpiece, becoming incongruously the most technically innovative yet ideologi-
cally retrograde film of its day.

Despite its intellectual dishonesty, or perhaps because of it, *Birth of
a Nation* was a commercial success. The movie broke all box-office
records despite boycotts by the NAACP and other black groups. And so
Hollywood, seeing the commercial jackpot plantation sagas might provide, began translating books and plays into screen epics. The embrace of
Southern apologism by Northern audiences coincided with the flowering
of American cinema—as celluloid supplanted the printed page, the
plantation, locus of literary and historical memory, became the perfect
vehicle for exploring American dreams.

Millions of Americans have had their vision of the South, race relations, and even the entire panorama of our past shaped if not wholly defined by the movie business. When nickelodeons began to attract audiences, the floods of immigrants eagerly sought flickering entertainments. The generation of immigrants who dominated American filmmaking through the Hollywood studios had a romantic attachment to the plantation legend. Al Jolson found his success in "minstrel" nostalgia, in blackface on his knees crooning "Mammy"—in the strange career of *The Jazz Singer* (1927). Film moguls followed—Sam Goldwyn, Louis B. Mayer, Jack Warner, and especially David O. Selznick. The "Southern" became a studio staple between the stock market crash in 1929 and America's entry into World War II, Hollywood's so-called golden age.

More than seventy genuine Southerns were produced. In the tradition of the Western, the Southern includes movies not merely set in the South but ones in which the South itself, or the idea of the South, played an integral role in the drama; the setting was not just a way to provide local color but became a force within the film. These movies found a tremendous audience outside the relatively unpopulated South. Indeed when cinema began its dizzying ascent, most Americans lived in the industrial Midwest and the commercialized Northeast. As late as 1930 the South had fewer than 4,000 movie houses that could seat less than two million viewers, as opposed to more than 17,500 theaters outside the area with a capacity of around eleven million. Although African

CELEBRATING THE KU KLUX KLAN IN A SCENE FROM *BIRTH OF A NATION* (1915).

Americans of every region were maligned by this genre, Southerns were projected as entertainment for all Americans. Movie studios shrugged off critics and cranked out more vehicles with demeaning stereotypic portraits of blacks and race relations. The seemingly limitless appetite of white Americans for the plantation epic encouraged studios to ignore black protests in favor of white ticket sales. When *Gone With the Wind* appeared in 1939, it lured record numbers of Americans to the box office. And Scarlett O'Hara became the most visible symbol of America's love affair with the Old South.

In 1946, a year of peak theater attendance in America, Walt Disney released *Song of the South*—a film replete with verdant plantations, cotton picking, and singing black folk. But this animated version of Joel Chandler Harris's popular Uncle Remus tales was perhaps the last gasp of the silver screen's plantation epic. World War II signalled a new era in which the postwar generation struggled to repackage if not revise outdated racist perspectives. Studios turned instead to "modern" Southern settings, which nonetheless reflected identically distorted racial views, if in a more sophisticated framework. One exception, the film version of Robert Penn Warren's *Band of Angels* (1957), was set in the Old South

A DEGRADING PUBLICITY STUNT FOR *GONE WITH THE WIND*, CIRCA 1950.

STEAMY INTERRACIAL ENCOUNTERS ARE A CENTRAL FEATURE OF SEXPLOITATION PLANTATION EPICS, EXEMPLIFIED BY HAMMOND (PERRY KING), THE PLANTER'S SON, AND ELLEN (BRENDA SYKES), HIS SLAVE AND BEDMATE, IN *MANDINGO* (1975).

and covered familiar territory, but with its portrait of miscegenation and its sympathetic mixed-race heroine, this film constituted a radical departure from earlier ventures.

The goal of the post–World War II Southern was to find new territory to explore without rocking traditions. The movie industry in this era often depicted the South as a tropical, languid region where hot-blooded people were stimulated to commit passionate, often immoral acts. Audiences wholeheartedly embraced this fiction. From *All the King's Men* (1949) to *Walk on the Wild Side* (1961), movies depicting corrupt Southern politics stirred up strong popular responses. *A Streetcar Named Desire* (1951), *Cat on a Hot Tin Roof* (1958), and *The Long Hot Summer* (1958) also wallowed in Southern sensuality.

This stylized image of the South did not remain unchallenged in the postwar era as serious cinema began to grapple with racial realities. The world and its racial climate were shifting. The landmark Supreme Court decision, *Brown v. Board of Education* (1954), struck down racial segregation in public education, and black veterans returning home from World War II began to seek the freedom and justice they had fought for abroad. As civil disobedience, sit-ins, and marches grew in the next decade, wouldn't the exaggerated fictions of the plantation epic necessarily disappear? Indeed several important films set in the South provided powerful contrast to sentimental tales: *The Defiant Ones* (1958), *To Kill a Mockingbird* (1963), and *In the Heat of the Night* (1967).

Although some Hollywood speculators continued to rework the plantation epic—most successfully in *Mandingo,* one of the top money-making films of 1975—by the late 1970s this genre, generally speaking, had faded from the big screen. It was reborn, however, on television, when Alex Haley's enormously successful epic, *Roots,* was made into a television miniseries in 1977. Its success fueled a stampede of less-skilled imitations, among them *Freedom Road, Beulahland, The Blue and the Gray, Charleston,* and *North and South* (Parts I, II, and III). Haley's posthumously televised return to the genre, *Queen* (1993), proved a ratings success, and the financial triumph of *Scarlett* has spawned plans for yet another sequel to the frequently rerun *Gone With the Wind.*

As celluloid—and video—versions of Southern stereotypes are

RACIST CARICATURE PERSISTS THROUGHOUT THE TWENTIETH CENTURY — FROM THE TWO POSTCARDS FROM THE 1890S, TO THE BOTTOM CARD, A REPRODUCTION FROM THE 1990S, THAT WAS PURCHASED AT A SOUTHERN AIRPORT GIFT SHOP.

broadcast to new generations, nostalgic and equally offensive plantation memorabilia has created a boom industry. Ceramic figurines, rag
dolls, Christmas tree ornaments, candles, old-fashioned collectibles,
and other modern artifacts are manufactured by the thousands and
sold all over the country as well as the South. These are not pieces
of material culture preserved to remind us of our past, but stylized representations of a misremembered past that are too often sold at the price
of African-American dignity. Sambo and, more often, Mammy make
their appearance in catalogs and antique doll displays in store windows
hawking "Americana." Some merchants display postcards and sign-
boards from the past that prominently feature racist language—"coon"
this and "nigger" that—often accompanied by repellent caricatures
involving watermelons or alligators.

Although sensitivity to race has caused many Americans to consider the consequences of perpetuating such images and to reconsider
owning, buying, and selling them, profit rules in the marketplace.
When traders are challenged, most plead absolute ignorance. I once
confronted a store owner in Kansas City, Missouri, concerning a candle
portraying a kneeling, grinning black boy offering up a
tray of fruit. When I asked if she thought such an item
was offensive, the shopkeeper replied that it wasn't
a candle at all but a "collectible." She was preserving
African-American "primitivism," she claimed, not promoting white racism.

Yet despite our assumptions, and the powerful
evidence in front of our eyes, the nature of these issues
is never as simple, as black and white, as it seems.
Anyone who thinks *Gone With the Wind*'s commercial
success was won at the price of black pride is confronted with Hattie McDaniel's brilliant performance,
which earned her an Academy Award in 1939—the
first Oscar awarded to a black actor. Indeed, the
producer David O. Selznick consulted with the
NAACP about the script to circumvent protests,
and courted black favor while filming the project.

If we dismiss widespread affection for Selznick's
film, its characters, and its settings, and see the story

CHRISTMAS TREE ORNAMENT OF PRISSY, A SLAVE CHARACTER FROM
GONE WITH THE WIND, PURCHASED IN AN ATLANTA GIFT SHOP IN 1994.

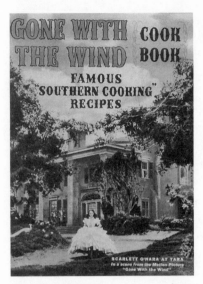

and its impact as mere nostalgia for slavery, we are reducing a complex formula of art, commerce, hype, and history to its lowest common—and most divisive—denominator. Certainly some of the simplification is true: while most of us are transported by this dazzling image into the Southern past, some listen for the clanking of the chains while others can hear only the ringing of the cash register. By and large, though, this sort of simplification is almost as absurd as arguing that the plantation setting and racial subtexts of Margaret Mitchell's book and the film drawn from it are incidental to its popularity. Tara is not merely a setting for *Gone With the Wind,* but maintains an ambiguous role somewhere between a character and a symbol. How else can we explain the phenomenon of *Scarlett* (with its grandiose subtitle "The Sequel to Margaret Mitchell's *Gone With the Wind*")? Written by an author of modest success, the authorized sequel rocketed to the top of the bestseller list in 1991 where it remained for several months, snaring a record price for film rights. Even more astoundingly, Mitchell's own novel proceeded to reappear on the national bestseller list, *over fifty years* after it was published.

The text, the film, and the legends surrounding both beguile more than half a century after their creation. Not despite of, but because of Tara's mythic quality, we are drawn into its thrall. The legendary plantation Tara was not built of bricks and mortar. This mythic estate is a state of mind, a romanticized fixation of the American historical imagination. Its sentimental associations have rendered Tara a popular girl's name, along with Ashley—names that echo throughout the film and ring across contemporary schoolyards to remind us of the vibrant affection many hold for this bygone world.

The mass cultural embrace of the symbol of Tara and the story it

---

ABOVE: *Gone With the Wind Cookbook* SELLS TENS OF THOUSANDS OF COPIES IN ITS CURRENT EDITION, DEMONSTRATING THE BROAD COMMERCIAL APPEAL OF THIS TRADEMARK NAME.

evokes has generated an unprecedented commercial success, which has continued for well over half a century. Legend and colorful depiction blur into a series of icono- graphic images that appear in every con- ceivable corner of media and commerce. Despite the ap- proved creation of *Gone With the Wind*'s multimillion-dollar sequel, the keepers of the Margaret Mitchell flame are outraged at other manifestations of the commercialization and flagrant trashing of their heroine's pure prod- uct. Particularly offensive is an enterprising pay-by-the-minute com- pany that hawks phone sex by urging customers to dial T-A-R-A.

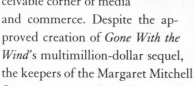

But the luminous figure of Scarlett O'Hara remains an incom- parable icon. O'Hara was the daughter of an immigrant, a man who had fulfilled the American dream by building his stake into a siz- able fortune to pass on to his family. During the Civil War, Gerald O'Hara invested his wealth in his beloved South, the pathos of his decline captured in the image of an old man clutching worthless Con- federate bonds. His wife Ellen died and his plantation lay in ruin. While Union victory ended his American dream, the saga continued. To O'Hara's plucky and invincible eldest daughter, Katie Scarlett, fell the burden of redeeming the family's fortunes. In the face of adver- sity—carpetbaggers, taxes, mercenary marriages, and melodramatic obstacles—Scarlett O'Hara was able to hang on to her land. Out of the ashes that was Twelve Oaks, the symbol of the dreamy, aristocratic South, Tara soars like a phoenix—reborn through the blood and sweat of a woman's determination and the labor she exploits.

O'Hara's tempestuous emotional upheavals, which drive the plot of *Gone With the Wind,* are, of course, central to the novel and film's popularity. But at the same time, Scarlett's near mystical attachment to

---

ABOVE: SCARLETT AND MAMMY SOUVENIRS DOUBLE AS BOTH MASKS AND FANS— MAKING THESE ITEMS IRONIC SYMBOLS OF RACIAL AMBIVALENCE.

the land remains an even more powerful theme. When all else fails her—when she has lost her beloved Melanie, her lust for Ashley, and has been deserted by Rhett Butler, whom she finally realizes she loves—Scarlett vows to go back to her homeplace, to return to Tara. In the book's textual and emotional context, we know this means a return to Mammy, whom Scarlett feels "will know what to do." Mammy and Tara, she believes, will always be there for her.

The image of Mammy nurtures the books' romantic escapism. Mitchell intended her as Scarlett's spiritual silhouette, and their symbiotic relationship forms the emotional core of the novel. Scarlett's starched petticoats represent hours of Mammy's labor and Scarlett's wasp waist (a direct contrast to Mammy's girth) is a product of Mammy's tight lacing. After Ellen O'Hara's death, Scarlett's conscience can only be supplicated through scolding and cajoling by her black surrogate mother, the indomitable mammy. Whatever strides we have made in the area of race relations, however many black Miss Americas may have reigned, Mammy remains. She lurks in the recesses, hidden in our cupboards. Smiling down from her box of pancake mix, Mammy remains whether she wears the traditional bandanna or the tastefully updated jewelry of the "new improved" Aunt Jemima. She is not just a nostalgic advertising ploy nor a cinematic artifact, but a force deeply linked to our embrace of plantation legend, our remembrance of things imagined. As we see Scarlett, in the foreground, sweeping down her oak-lined drive, Mammy remains, in the background, but still within sight.

No matter how comforting and familiar these images may be, they remain fictional rather than historical representations. To recapture the experiences of real women remains a powerful draw. The imprisonment of Rose Greenhow, the hospital hardships of Phoebe Pember and Kate Cumming, the daring espionage of Mary Elizabeth Bowser, the extraordinary feats of Harriet Tubman, the vivid exploits of Belle Boyd, all these and more deepen and enrich our appreciation of Southern women's wartime experiences. The poignant letters of Jane Pickett, a refugee en route from Mississippi to Georgia, and the touching reminiscences of Susie King Taylor en route from slavery to freedom demonstrate the wide range of documentary sources available to illuminate women's endurance and adventure. The sagas of Mary Boykin Chesnut, Ella Gertrude Thomas, and so many other vivid Confederate women diarists supply us with complex narratives that continue to fascinate academic and popular audiences alike.

Whatever "truths" these real women reveal provoke as much controversy as those images steeped in stereotype and tinted with romanticism. Southern women may never emerge from the trappings of myth and nostalgia, but by systematically exploring the lives behind those images, the thorns as well as the blossoms, our historical understanding will broaden, deepen, and eventually reshape our perceptions of the plantation era. In this way we can revitalize the Southern past, expanding significantly our appreciation of the sexual dynamics of sectionalism and the gender conflicts reconfigured by war.

The belle and mammy images, so persistently yoked, will continue to shape our views of Southern women, exerting great influence whether we confront them or not. But just as scholarly and cultural trends shift over time, perhaps there will be a waning interest in these distorted if splendid myths. Whitewashed renditions of Americans at war may be replaced by bold and dramatic new tales, culled from evidence now gathering dust—letters handed down through families who lived in cabins as well as mansions.

Our stake in America's plantation heritage continues to haunt as we wrangle over its meanings, its sentimentalism and sins, its legacy today. After countless debates and exhaustive deconstructions, it is hard to tell what we are left with. Yet certain legends endure. Tara remains contested yet transcendent—bewildering, unbending, and beguiling. And its distinctive, compelling image prods us to re-examine a fascinating crossroads of history and memory, beckoning us to revisit, yet again, another day.

References

References

A vast array of primary sources is available on plantation life during the Civil War. Several dozen published journals and collections of women's letters and family documents remain in print. Among my favorites are Carol Bleser, *The Hammonds of Redcliffe* (New York: Oxford University Press, 1981); Virginia Burr, *The Secret Eye: The Journal of Ella Gertrude Clanton Thomas* (Chapel Hill: University of North Carolina Press, 1990); Charles East, *Civil War Diary of Sarah Morgan* (Athens: University of Georgia Press, 1991); Robert Manson Myers, *The Children of Pride* (New Haven: Yale University Press, 1972); Mary Robertson, *Lucy Breckenridge of Grove Hill* (Kent, Ohio: Kent State University Press, 1979); Camilla Travis Trammell, *Seven Pines* (Dallas: Southern Methodist University Press, 1986); C. Vann Woodward, *Mary Chesnut's Civil War* (New Haven: Yale University Press, 1981); and Patricia Romero, *A Black Woman's Civil War Memoirs* [Susie King Taylor] (New York: Marcus Wiener Publishing, 1988). Two important scholarly series make available significant sources on southern women: The Schomburg Library of Nineteenth-Century Black Women Writers (Oxford University Press), edited by Henry Louis Gates, Jr., and Carol Bleser's series for the University of Georgia Press, Southern Voices From the Past: Women's Letters, Diaries, and Writings.

I have benefited from the work of dozens of scholars in the field, but remain grateful for the work of Anne Firor Scott, Jacqueline Jones, George Rable, LeeAnn Whites, Pauli Murray, Drew Gilpin Faust, Dorothy Sterling, Mary E. Massey, and especially Katharine M. Jones,

PAGES 214–15: RICE RAFT, GEORGETOWN, SOUTH CAROLINA.

whose pioneering editing and prolific publications have provided me with terrific background during this project. I have also learned much from the dozens of works I cite in the notes below.

Hundreds of thousands of unpublished letters and journals are deposited in archives throughout the nation, but primarily in the South, where treasure troves and legendary hospitality are commonplace. Here is a list of the most useful sources, followed by their abbreviations:

Alabama State Archives, Montgomery (ASA)

Atlanta Historical Society (AHS)

Collection of Writings by Virginia Women, Randolph-Macon Woman's College, Lynchburg, Virginia (RMWC)

Duke University, Durham, North Carolina (DU)

Filson Club, Louisville, Kentucky (FC)

Mississippi State Archives, Jackson (MSA)

Museum of the Confederacy, Richmond, Virginia (MOC)

Records of the Bureau of Refugees, Freedman and Abandon Lands,

National Archives, Washington, D.C. (BRF&AL)

Southern Historical Collection, University of North Carolina, Chapel Hill (SHC)

United Daughters of the Confederacy, Richmond, Virginia (UDC)

University of South Carolina, Columbia (SCL)

University of Virginia, Charlottesville (UVA)

Virginia Historical Society, Richmond (VHS)

Virginia State Library, Richmond (VSL)

Washington and Lee College, Lexington, Virginia (W&L)

Archives across the nation also contain hundreds of compelling images, many of which have been reproduced in this volume. The best repositories for visual material in the field remain:

Museum of the Confederacy, Richmond, Virginia (MOC)

Valentine Museum, Richmond, Virginia (VM)

Atlanta Historical Society (AHS)

Virginia Historical Society, Richmond (VHS)

National Archives, Washington, D.C. (NA)

New-York Historical Society, New York (NYHS)

Library of Congress, Washington, D.C. (LC)

Historic New Orleans (HNO)

Motion Picture Academy of Arts and Sciences, Hollywood, California (MPAAS)

The Museum of Modern Art, New York (MoMA)

Virginia Military Institute, Lexington (VMI)

South Carolina Historical Society, Charleston (SCHS)

South Carolina History and Relic Room, Columbia (SCR)

Randolph Macon Woman's College, Lynchburg, Virginia (RMWC)

U.S. Military History Institute, Carlisle, Pennsylvania (USMHI)

Notes

OF LEGENDS AND PLANTATIONS

p. 18, "For every Southern boy . . ."
William Faulkner, *Intruder in the Dust*
(New York: Random House, 1948),
p. 194.

p. 19, For the cult of the Lost Cause, see
Charles R. Wilson, *Baptized in Blood:
The Religion of the Lost Cause, 1865–
1920* (Athens: University of Georgia
Press, 1980) and Gaines Foster, *Ghosts
of the Confederacy: Defeat, the Lost
Cause and the Emergence of the New
South, 1865–1913* (New York: Oxford
University Press, 1987).

BEFORE FORT SUMTER

p. 29, "that the plantation can never flourish . . ." Julia Cherry Spruill, *Women's
Life and Work in the Southern Colonies* (Chapel Hill: University of North
Carolina, 1938), p. 9.

p. 30, "I find it requires a great care . . ."
Constance Schultz, "Eliza Lucas
Pinckney," in G. J. Barket-Benfield
and Catherine Clinton, *Portraits of
American Women* (New York: St.
Martin's Press, 1991), p. 77.

p. 31, "I have been six months . . ."
Catherine Clinton, *The Other Civil
War: American Women in the Nine-
teenth Century* (New York: Hill and
Wang, 1984), p. 4.

p. 31, "A white woman . . ." Robert Beverly, *The History and Present State
of Virginia,* reprint of 1722 edition
(Chapel Hill: University of North
Carolina, 1947), p. 211.

p. 31, "Approximately ten thousand

slaves . . ." Peter Wood, "Impatient of
Oppression: Black Freedom Struggles on the Eve of White Independence," *Southern Exposure* 12, no. 6
(1984), p. 13.

p. 33, "separated from parents by the age
of six . . ." Betty Wood, "Some Aspects of Female Resistance to Chattel
Slavery in Low Country Georgia,"
Historical Journal 30, no. 3 (1987),
p. 68.

p. 34, "The women who visited me . . ."
Frances Anne Kemble, *Journal of
Residence on a Georgian Plantation in
1838–1839 by Frances Anne Kemble,*
ed. John A. Scott (New York: Knopf,
1961), p. 222.

p. 34, "the people on this plantation . . ."
Kemble, *Journal of Residence,* p. 229.

p. 37, "I now entered on my fifteenth
year . . ." Harriet Jacobs [Linda Brent,
pseud.], *Incidents in the Life of a Slave
Girl,* ed. Jean Yellin (Cambridge,
Mass.: Harvard University Press,
1986), p. 27.

p. 37, "Mr. K[ing] forced her . . ." Kemble, *Journal of Residence,* p. 199.

p. 38, "slipped in a colored gal's room . . ."
George Rawick, ed., *The American
Slave* (Westport, Conn.: Greenwood
Press, 1972), vol. 13, p. 4.

p. 41, "While the husband took care of the
land . . ." Catherine Clinton, *Plantation Mistress: Woman's World in the Old
South* (New York: Pantheon, 1982),
p. 22.

p. 41, "The mistress of a plantation . . ."
Susan Dabney Smedes, *Memorials of a*

Southern Planter (New York: Knopf, 1965), p. 179.

p. 43, "It is a fault in female education ..." Clinton, *Plan: ʾ+ion Mistress,* p. 19.

p. 43, "for the first time ..." Letitia Burwell, *A Girl's Life in Virginia Before the War* (New York: Frederick A. Stockes, 1895), p. 23.

p. 43, "Now I have turned housekeeper ..." Mary Withers to Ann Eliza Withers, June 25, 1831, Leveret Papers, SHC.

p. 44, "For whatever you may think ..." Clinton, *Plantation Mistress,* p. 179.

MARCHING OFF TO WAR

p. 53, "I cannot see a shadow ..." Robert Manson Myers, *The Children of Pride* (New Haven, Conn.: Yale University Press, 1972), p. 627.

p. 53, "These foolish, rash, harebrained ..." Mary Boykin Chesnut, *Mary Chesnut's Civil War,* C. Vann Woodward, ed. (New Haven, Conn.: Yale University Press, 1981), p. 128.

p. 54, "The Question under discussion ..." Mary Louise Reid to Samuel Reid, February 28, 1861, Lexington, Virginia, Mary L. White Collection, W&L.

p. 55, "The happiness of your life ..." Clinton, *Plantation Mistress,* p. 44.

p. 56, "enthusiasm which had not been witnessed ..." Jane Pickett to her sister, August 1861, Boddie Family Papers, MSA.

p. 56, "I never fully realized ..." Septima M. Collis, *A Woman's War*

Record, *1861–1865* (New York: G. P. Putnam's Sons, 1889), pp. 18–19.

p. 56, "I never go in Public ..." H. E. Sterkx, *Partners in Rebellion* (Rutherford, N.J.: Farleigh Dickinson University Press, 1970), p. 34.

p. 57, "Almost every girl plaits her own hat ..." Judith Brockenbrough McGuire in Katherine Jones, *Ladies of Richmond* (Indianapolis: Bobbs-Merrill, 1962), p. 152.

p. 60, "Can you imagine ..." Drew Faust, "Altars of Sacrifice," in Catherine Clinton and Nina Silber, *Divided Houses: Gender and the Civil War* (New York: Oxford University Press, 1992), p. 175.

p. 60, "kept up splendid ..." Fannie A. Beers, *Memories: A Record of Experiences During Four Years of War* (Philadelphia: J. B. Lippincott Co., 1891).

p. 61, "hurl the destructive novel in the fire ..." from April 25, 1861, *Augusta Chronicle & Sentinel.*

p. 61, "This great sorrow makes me feel ..." Diary of Mary Williamson, ASA.

p. 62, "they may have to exterminate us ..." Augusta Kollock to her brother, January 22, 1861, Chatham County, Georgia, in Katharine M. Jones, ed., *Heroines of Dixie* (Indianapolis: Bobbs-Merrill, 1955).

p. 62, "The ladies trimmed Estelle Hall ..." Eleanor Noyes Jackson, February 19, 1861, Montgomery, Alabama, in Jones, *Heroines of Dixie,* p. 13.

p. 62, "All yesterday evening . . ." Emma Holmes diary, April 13, 1861, in Jones, *Heroines of Dixie,* p. 19.

p. 64, "With a sad heavy heart . . ." Mary Custis Lee, April 20, 1861, Arlington, Virginia, in Jones, *Heroines of Dixie,* p. 24.

p. 64, "Mrs. General Lee has been with us . . ." Judith Brockenbrough McGuire, June 5, 1861, in Jones, *Heroines of Dixie,* p. 44.

p. 64, "the most dreary state . . ." Woodward, *Mary Chesnut's Civil War,* p. 117.

p. 65, "Companies in dress parade . . ." Jane Pickett to her sister, August 12, 1861, Montgomery White Sulpher Springs, Virginia, Boddie Family Papers, MSA.

p. 65, "Oh! Alice, you cannot be thankful enough . . ." Lallie to Alice Bailey Boozer, October 31, 1862, Boozer Collection, SCL.

p. 65, "Let us not be discouraged . . ." Lucy Johnston Ambler, July 16 [n.a.], MS Collection 5191, UVA.

p. 66, "We went to Clay Hill . . ." Mathella Page Harrison, January 12, 1862, MS Collection 9751, UVA.

p. 66, "Fashion is an obsolete word . . ." Kate Stone, *Brockenburn: The Journal of Kate Stone,* ed. John Q. Anderson (Baton Rouge: Louisiana State University Press, 1955), p. 109.

p. 69, "In our late expedition . . ." Harriet Tubman in C. Peter Ripley, ed., *Witness for Freedom: African-American Voices on Race, Slavery, and Emancipation* (Chapel Hill: University of North Carolina Press, 1993), pp. 244–45.

p. 71, "we snook out of de house . . ." Dorothy Sterling, *We Are Your Sisters: Black Women in the Nineteenth Century* (New York: W. W. Norton, 1984), p. 238.

p. 71, "General, dese han's never . . ." Sterling, *We Are Your Sisters,* p. 239.

p. 72, "They are treating me worse and worse every day . . ." Berlin et al., *Freedom: A Documentary History of Emancipation,* vol. II (New York: Cambridge University Press), p. 686.

p. 72, "A practice had largely obtained among owners . . ." Berlin et al., *Freedom,* p. 686.

p. 73, "my respects is worn out . . ." Berlin et al., *Freedom,* p. 689.

p. 74, "who told me that if I did not go back . . ." Berlin et al., *Freedom,* p. 695.

THOSE WHO SERVED

p. 79, "What the event will be of the present secession . . ." Jane Pickett to her sister, February 1, 1861, Benton, Yazoo County, Mississippi. Boddie Family Papers, MSA.

p. 80, "Have you not often seen my anxiety . . ." David Campbell to Maria Campbell, January 3, 1823, Campbell Collection, DU.

p. 83, "a sleepless vigil by day and night . . ." Sterkx, *Partners in Rebellion,* p. 115.

p. 83, "The ladies in town have been preparing . . ." Mary Louise Reid to Samuel Reid, October 19, 1861, Lexington, Virginia, Mary L. White Collection, W&L.

p. 83, "The surgeon-general has informed me . . ." Sterkx, *Partners in Rebellion,* p. 114.

p. 83, "I sent you a letter the other day . . ." Kate Kern to Mrs. Presnell, October 2, 1864, Sea Green, Winchester, Virginia, Kate Kern Letters, MS Collection 30181, VSL.

p. 85, "some of her acquaintances from Rome . . ." Cornelia Kincaid to Alice Bailey, January 2, 1863, Oakley, Chattanooga County, Georgia, Boozer Collection, SCL.

p. 85, "It is now nearly 2 o'clock Sunday night . . ." Sally Tompkins to her sister Ellen, July 22, 1861, Arlington House, Tompkins Collection 24395, VSL.

p. 87, "Other vermin, the change of seasons would rid us of..." Phoebe Yates Pember in B. A. Botkin, *Civil War Treasury of Tales, Legends and Folklore* (New York: Random House, 1960), p. 147.

p. 88, "Four of our sick died that night..." Fannie A. Beers, *Memories: A Record of Experiences During Four Years of War* (Philadelphia: J. B. Lippincott Co., 1891), p. 117.

p. 88, "the men are lying all over the house..." April 12, 1862, Jones, *Heroines of Dixie*, p. 110.

p. 88, "As I passed by the rows of occupied cots..." Sarah Rice Pryor, MS Collection 24061, VSL.

p. 88, "Can't you wait until we are dead?" Jennie D. Harrold, in Jones, *Ladies of Richmond*, p. 134.

p. 88, "The last few days he lived..." L. Selina Johnson, "One Story of the Civil War: The Second Battle of Bull Run" (1898), UDC.

p. 91, "Some of our best..." Bell Wiley, *The Life of Johnny Reb: The Common Soldier of the Confederacy* (Indianapolis: Bobbs-Merrill, 1943), p. 55.

p. 91, "I began to fix my articles for smuggling..." Belle Edmondson, March 16, 1864, MS Collection 1707, SHC.

p. 91, "I am strangely laden..." Malvina Black Gist diary, February 15, 1865, SCL.

p. 92, "One lady had seven pairs of gaiters..." *Raleigh Weekly Register,* March 3, 1863, p. 2.

p. 93, "of bad repute and recognized..." Mary Massey, *Bonnet Brigades: American Women in the Civil War* (New York: Knopf, 1966), p. 91.

p. 99, Emma Edmonds. See Lyde Cullen Sizer, "Acting Her Part: Narratives of Union Women Spies" in Clinton and Silber, *Divided Houses,* p. 124.

p. 100, "My enjoyment—if I can designate..." Loreta Janeta Velazquez, *The Woman in Battle: A Narrative of the Exploits, Adventures and Travels of Madame Loreta Janeta Velazquez...* (Hartford, Conn., 1876).

p. 101, "Richmond was greatly shocked on Friday..." Massey, *Bonnet Brigades,* p. 148.

p. 102, "common camp followers..." Bell Wiley, *Life of Johnnie Reb,* p. 54.

p. 103, "I remember what a roar..." Susie King Taylor, *A Black Woman's Civil War Memoirs: Reminiscences of My Life in Camp with the 33rd United States Colored Troops, Late 1st S.C. Volunteers,* reprint of 1902 ed. (New York: Arno Press, 1968), p. 33.

p. 103, "I learned to handle a musket very well..." Taylor, *Memoirs,* p. 26.

p. 104, "There are many people who do not know what some..." Taylor, *Memoirs,* p. 26.

THOSE WHO ALSO SERVED: BACK ON THE LAND

p. 110, "Dear Madam:... " Botkin, *Civil War Treasury,* p. 373.

p. 111, "Accompanied by every act of cruelty..." Francis W. Dawson, *Our Women in the War* (Charleston, S.C.: Walker, Evans & Cogswell Company, 1887), p. 23.

p. 112, "the real sorrows of war..." George Cary Eggleston, *A Rebel's Recollections* (New York: Hurd & Houghton, 1875).

p. 112, "To feed, to clothe, to teach..." Dawson, *Our Women,* p. 12.

p. 112, "South Carolina as a rule..." Woodward, *Mary Chesnut,* p. 569.

p. 112, "Such pictures of horrors..." Margaret Junkin Preston, *Life and Letters of Margaret Junkin Preston* (Boston: Houghton Mifflin, 1903), Elizabeth Allan, ed., p. 149.

p. 112, "I feel 10 years older..." Louisa Henry to her mother, Arcadia,

April 28, 1862[?], Boddie Family Papers, MSA.

p. 113, "Were these same people—these haggard . . ." Dawson, *Our Women,* p. 17.

p. 113, "What a change has passed over my life . . ." Amanda Worthington, Worthington Collection, MSA.

p. 113, "I do not think I am so much more sinful . . ." Mary Vaughn to her sister, February 22, 1863, Sunny Side, Boddie Family Papers, MSA.

p. 115, "he has done all our hawling . . ." Petition to governor, n.d., signed by seventeen women, Papers of Governor Andrew G. Magrath, SCA.

p. 115, "Do not call me unpatriotic . . ." Clara Bowen to Alice Bailey, February 13, 1864, Boozer Collection, SCL.

p. 116, "Later on when the work of keeping . . ." Louisa McCord Smythe diary, typescript, p. 52, SCHS.

p. 117, "I wish some of those persons at the North . . ." Charlotte Forten, *Journals of Charlotte Forten,* Brenda Stevenson, ed. (New York: Oxford University Press, 1988), p. 397.

p. 118, "I want to sell and go . . ." Unidentified sister of Louisa Henry [1861], Boddie Family Papers, MSA.

p. 118, "I have never thought of being afraid . . ." Woodward, *Mary Chesnut,* p. 199.

p. 118, "I intend to get Mr. Downs . . ." Lucy Johnston Ambler diary, February 21, 1863, Morven, Farquier County, Virginia, MS 5191, UVA.

p. 119, "It has gotten to be very common with the darkies . . ." Melissa Fooshe, January 25, 1863, Fouche Family Collection, SCL.

p. 119, "those we loved best . . ." Myrta Lockett Avary, *Dixie After the War* (New York: D. Appleton & Co., 1903), p. 263.

p. 120, "Do you want to go to the Yan-

kees? . . ." Flora McDonald Williams, W*ho's the Patriot? A Story of the Southern Confederacy* (Louisville, Ky.: Courier Journal Printing Company, 1886), p. 178.

p. 120, "A family of negroes . . ." Belle Edmondson Diary, February 15, 1864, Shelby City, Tennessee, MS Collection 1707, SHC.

p. 121, "in some cases have left the plantation . . ." Jane Pickett to her mother, July 25, 1863, Montevallo, Boddie Family Papers, MSA.

p. 121, "The wife of a colored recruit . . ." Berlin et al., *Freedom,* p. 688.

p. 121, "The field negroes are in a dreadful state . . ." Emma LeConte, February 1865, Pooshee Plantation in Berkeley County, South Carolina, SHC.

p. 121, see Mary Cary Ambler Stribling, April 1862, MS 25390, VSL.

p. 121, "was forced to go out into the woods . . ." Sallie Brock, *Richmond During the War* (Alexandria, Va.: Time-Life Books, 1983), p. 166.

p. 122, "My heart has yearned . . ." Louisa Henry to her mother, March 28, 1864, Arcadia, Mississippi, Boddie Family Papers, MSA.

p. 122, "We had even cut up our carpets . . ." Sallie Moore, *Memories of a Long Life in Virginia* (Staunton, Va.: McClure Company, 1920), p. 70.

p. 122, "in case of your being sick . . ." Louisa S. McCord to "My dear young friend," August 20, 1863, Columbia, McCord Collection, SCL.

p. 122, "the ground has been covered . . ." Rebecca Ridley, December 18, 1864, Jefferson, Tennessee, in Jones, *Heroines of Dixie,* p. 350.

p. 122, "I told ma when *provisions* . . ." Katie Miller to her aunt, April 3, 1864, French Camp, Boddie Family Papers, MSA.

p. 122, "the creature selected for this

business..." *Charleston Daily Courier,* January 8, 1862, p. 4.

p. 123, "They tore the ear rings . . ." Cordelia Lewis Scales, January 27, 1863, "Destructive Hollow, Mississippi," in Jones, *Heroines of Dixie,* p. 220.

p. 123, Amanda Worthington papers, Worthington Collection, MSA.

p. 123, "Yankees stripped us bare . . ." Mary Ann Huff, "The Role of Women in Confederate Georgia" (M.A. thesis, Vanderbilt University, 1967), p. 70.

p. 123, "But like demons..." Dolly Lunt, November 19, 1864, Huff, "The Role of Women," p. 72.

p. 123, "They came into the house . . ." Mary Cary Ambler Stribling, May 1862, Fort Royal, Virginia, MS 25390, VSL.

p. 124, "then another, but before . . ." Memoir of Ella Hard, Collection of Charles F. Hard, SCL.

p. 124, "would these great champions of liberty . . ." Madam S. Sosnowski, "Scenes and Incident During the Burning of Columbia," South Carolina, UDC Scrapbook, vol. 58, p. 6, MOC.

p. 124, "I was in *mortal* terror . . ." Louisa Henry to her mother, March 28, 1864, Arcadia, Mississippi, Boddie Family Papers, VSL.

p. 125, "Your name will stand . . ." Henrietta Lee from Matthew Page Andrews, *The Women of the South in Wartime* (Baltimore: Remington Company, 1927), p. 127.

p. 125, "suddenly a string broke . . ." Moore, *Memories of a Long Life,* p. 69.

p. 125, "there was a loud rapping . . ." "Reminiscences of Susan Olmsted," Savannah, Georgia, typescript, pp. 1–3, VSL.

p. 126, "I was nursin' my baby . . ." Eliza

Sparks, in Sterling, *We Are Your Sisters,* p. 242.

p. 127, For Nora Canning, see Dawson, *Our Women in the War,* p. 21.

p. 127, "Mrs. M. R. Fort was a lady . . ." *Raleigh Register,* September 19, 1863.

p. 129, "out of twenty-two executions for rape . . ." See Robert Alotta, *Civil War Justice: Union Army Executions Under Lincoln* (Shippensburg, Pa.: White Mane Publishing Company, 1989), p. 19.

p. 129, "The case of Mr. Shane's old Negro woman . . ." Daniel Heywards Trezevant in Rod Gragg, *Illustrated Confederate Reader* (New York: Harper & Row, 1989), p. 192.

p. 130, "Mrs. G. told me of a young lady . . ." Trezevant in Gragg, *Illustrated Confederate Reader,* p. 192.

p. 130, "this is all the money I have in the world . . ." Clara D. MacLean, "The Last Raid," *Southern Historical Society Papers* 12 (1885): pp. 466–76.

p. 131, See letters of Jane Pickett to her mother and sister, Jane Pickett, Boddie Family Papers, MSA.

p. 132, "Separated from those dear members . . ." Capt. L. N. Buck and Mary Rowe, eds., *Diary of Lucy Rebecca Buck, 1861–1865. Front Royal, Virginia* (Baltimore, Md., 1940), p. 25.

p. 132, "I ran upstairs..." Emma LeConte diary, February 17, 1865, Columbia, South Carolina, LeConte Collection, SHC.

p. 133, "These were trying times . . ." Virginia McCollum Stinson in Jones, *Heroines of Dixie,* p. 274.

p. 133, "Well, in truth, I think . . ." Mary Wall to Shelly, May 1, 1864, Orange City, Virginia, MS 10482, UVA.

p. 134, See Eliza Frances [Fanny] Andrews, *The War-Time Journal of a Georgia Girl, 1864–65* (New York: D. Appleton & Co., 1908), p. 112.

p. 134, For Ella Gertrude Clanton

Thomas, see *The Secret Eye: The Journal of Ella Gertrude Canton Thomas,* ed. *Virginia Burr* (Chapel Hill: University of North Carolina Press, 1990).

p. 135, Narcissa Black, in *Black Belt to Hill Country: Alabama Quilts* (Birmingham, Ala.: Birmingham Museum of Art, 1981).

THE CULT OF SACRIFICE

p. 139, "Do the annals of any country ..." *Confederate Scrapbook* (Richmond, Va.: J. L. Hill, 1893), p. 56 (RMWC).

p. 140, "Let us work for them ..." Maria Louisa Fleet in Betsy Fleet, ed., *Green Mount After the War* (Charlottesville: University of Virginia Press, 1978), p. 9.

p. 140, For the Bells of North Carolina, see Dawson, *Our Women in the War,* p. 18.

p. 141, "I am not interested in Rebel wives . . ." Lee Meriwether memoir, UDC.

p. 142, "In times to come ..." Botkin, *Civil War Treasury,* pp. 250–51.

p. 142, "Fold away all your bright-tinted dresses . . ." Dawson, *Our Women in the War,* p. 6.

p. 143, "to assist in redeeming the currency . . ." Sterkx, *Partners in Rebellion,* p. 85.

p. 143, "Let every patriotic woman's head . . ." Sterkx, *Partners in Rebellion,* p. 85.

p. 144, "Several of us are engaged in making soap . . ." Judith Brockenbrough McGuire, *Diary of a Southern Refugee During the War* (New York: E. J. Hale and Son, 1868), p. 67.

p. 144, "I did not have a cake . . ." Carrie Berry diary, Atlanta, Georgia, AHS.

p. 144, "I have seen little . . ." Emma LeConte, February 1865, SHC.

p. 145, "I think the war is teaching us ..." Amanda Worthington diary, MSA.

p. 145, "The Yankees are coming to our house ..." Cornelia Peake McDonald, June 11, 1864, in Jones, *Heroines of Dixie,* p. 306.

p. 145, "A lovely little girl of six ..." Dawson, *Our Women in the War,* p. 18.

p. 145, "When they rose from breakfast . . ." Cornelia Peake McDonald, June 11, 1864, Jones, *Heroines of Dixie,* p. 308.

p. 147, "Yes, Moses also viewed the promised land . . ." Mrs. S. G. Tinsley's War Experiences, UDC Scrapbooks, vol. 40, p. 113, MOC.

p. 147, "I had to stay here all by myself ..." Amanda Worthington diary, MSA.

p. 147, "G. and H. at Sally White's birthday . . ." Margaret Junkin Preston, *Life and Letters of Margaret Junkin Preston ed. Elizabeth Allan* (Boston: Houghton Mifflin, 1903), p. 233.

p. 148, "I went with the white chillun ..." Rachel Harris in Peter Bardaglio, "The Children of Jubilee: African-American Childhood in Wartime," Clinton and Silber, *Divided Houses,* p. 219.

p. 148, "You know chillun them days ..." James Henry Nelson in Bardaglio, "The Children of Jubilee," p. 221.

p. 148, "plowed a mule an' wild un at dat ..." Eliza Scantling in Bardaglio, "The Children of Jubilee," p. 221.

p. 148, "just one eye and dat right in de middle ..." Bardaglio, "The Children of Jubilee," p. 222.

p. 148, "it wuzn't nuthin' to fin' a dead man ..." James Goings in Bardaglio, "The Children of Jubilee," p. 223.

p. 148, "My daddy go 'way to de war ..." Amie Lumpkin in Bardaglio, "The Children of Jubilee," p. 225.

p. 149, "as many as six or eight wheels ..." Parthenia Antoinette Hague, in Jones, *Heroines of Dixie,* p. 265.

p. 149, "We were drawn together in a

closer union . . ." Parthenia Antoinette Hague, in Jones, *Heroines of Dixie,* p. 265.

p. 149, "democratic feasts those were . . ." Constance Cary in Jones, *Ladies of Richmond,* p. 92.

p. 149, "which soon, becoming thoroughly saturated with the melted lard . . ." Parthenia Hague, in Jones, *Heroines of Dixie,* p. 264.

p. 149, "I have a letter from my brother . . ." Louisa McCord Smythe memoir, typescript, p. 52, SCHS.

p. 150, "The fire was lit but burned out before morning . . ." Louisa McCord Smythe memoir, typescript, p. 53, SCHS.

p. 150, "Slowly but surely the south was 'bled white' . . ." Sarah Rice Pryor, Charlotte City, Virginia, MS Collection 24061, VSL.

p. 150, "Out shopping all morning . . ." Kate Sperry, September 3 (n.a.), MS Collection 28532, VSL.

p. 150, "Indeed everything looks very gloomy . . ." Lucy Johnston Ambler diary, August 3, 1863, Farquier City, Virginia, MS Collection 5191, UVA.

p. 151, "Food was frightfully scarce . . ." Louisa McCord Smythe memoir, typescript, p. 52, SCHS.

p. 151, "I knew women to walk twenty miles . . ." Miss A. C. Clark of Atlanta, in Dawson, *Our Women in the War,* p. 17.

p. 152, "We would have died before we would complain . . ." Louisa McCord Smythe memoir, SCHS.

p. 152, "My God! How can I pay such prices . . ." Botkin, *Civil War Treasury,* p. 253.

p. 152, "A white foam comes at first . . ." Susan Bradford, in Jones, *Heroines of Dixie,* p. 260.

p. 153, "We are starving . . ." Jones, *Ladies of Richmond,* p. 155.

p. 153, "I am telling you of it because . . ." Jones, *Ladies of Richmond,* p. 156.

p. 153, "I do not think the speculative spirit . . ." Virginia Cloud, April 22 [1863], Fort Royal, Virginia, Virginia Cloud diary, W&L.

p. 154, For the Shelton Laurel massacre, see Philip Paludan, *Victims* (Knoxville: University of Tennessee Press, 1981).

p. 154, "She came down with the expectation . . ." Melissa Fooshe, January 25, 1863, Ninety-Six, South Carolina, Fouche Family Collection, SCL.

p. 154, "prepare a girdle to be worn all the time . . ." Sarah Rice Pryor, MS Collection 24061, VSL.

p. 155, "This is indeed a terrible war . . ." Cousin Kit to Alice Bailey, May 13, 1863, Union, South Carolina, Boozer Collection, SCL.

p. 155, "And since the destruction of my own heart treasures . . ." Mildred to Lucy, April 1, 1865, MS Collection, 29881, VSL.

p. 155, "I am afraid that God will suffer . . ." Andrews, *War-Time Journal,* p. 211.

p. 156, "Our eyes were fastened upon it . . ." Mary Ann Loughborough, *My Cave Life in Vicksburg* (New York: D. Appleton, 1864), p. 115.

p. 158, "On returning, an explosion sounded near her . . ." Loughborough, in Jones, *Heroines of Dixie,* p. 234.

p. 159, "The great battles seem to move the Nation . . ." Virginia Cloud, January 17, 1863, Fort Royal, Virginia, Virginia Cloud diary, W&L.

AFTER APPOMATTOX

p. 163, "I had rather take to my heart . . ." Dawson, *Our Women and War,* p. 19.

p. 164, "I was in the kitchen getting breakfast . . ." Mathilda Dunbar, Sterling, *We Are Your Sisters,* p. 243.

p. 164, For the Jones family of Liberty County, see Robert Manson Myers, *The Children of Pride* (New Haven, Conn.: Yale University Press, 1972).

p. 166, For Wesleyan students, see Huff, "Role of Women in Confederate Georgia," p. 131.

p. 166, "Any where in the land, a Southern girl's . . ." Myrta Lockett Avary, *Dixie After the War,* p. 117.

p. 168, For Jefferson Davis's daughter, see Joan E. Cashin, "Varina Davis," Barker-Benfield and Clinton, *Portraits of American Women,* vol. 1, pp. 259–277.

p. 168, "We have one of the dear creatures . . ." Louisa McCord Smythe, May 28, 1865, Columbia, South Carolina, Louisa McCord Smythe Collection, SCL.

p. 169, "Last evening about 8 o'clock . . ." *Charleston Daily Courier,* September 22, 1865, p. 2.

p. 170, "The pinch of want is making itself felt . . ." Andrews, *War-Time Journal,* p. 119.

p. 170, "improvised a new social system . . ." Eggleston, *A Rebel's Recollection,* pp. 74–5.

p. 171, "I am a widow and before the war . . ." Mrs. A. G. Smith to Governor James Orr, July 12, 1866 (misfiled under July 17), Barnwell, South Carolina, Letters received, Governors correspondence, SCA.

p. 171, "You wish to know my plans . . ." April 24, 1867, Montgomery, Lide-Coker-Stout Family Collection, SCL.

p. 171, "I got your letter . . ." Jourdon Anderson in Botkin, *Civil War Treasury,* pp. 567–69.

p. 172, "All we had in the South is gone . . ." Letitia Preston Wallace to her son, April 20, 1865, Wallace Papers, FC.

p. 173, Frances Butler Leigh, *Ten Years on a Georgian Plantation Since the War* (London: Bentley & Sons, 1883), p. 35.

p. 173, Carol Bleser, "The Perrys of Greenville: A Nineteenth-Century Marriage," Fraser, Saunders and Wakelyn, eds., *The Web of Southern Social Relations: Women, Family and Education* (Athens: University of Georgia Press, 1985).

p. 174, "I heard the saddest thing the other day . . ." See unpublished essay by Michele Gillespie.

p. 174, "Our Amy was not a slave . . ." Henrietta Daingerfield, *Our Mammy and Other Stories* (Lexington, Ky., 1906), p. 27 (RMWC).

p. 175, "all felt very much mortified and hurt . . ." See Sallie Mae Dooley, *Dem Good Ole Days* (New York: Doubleday, Page & Co., 1906), p. 25.

p. 175, "The first greenbacks were brought to one family . . ." Avary, *Dixie After the War,* p. 150.

p. 176, "the fear of a negro could not cross the brains . . ." Delia Bryan Page, *Recollections of Home for My Brothers and Children* (Richmond: W. E. Jones, 1903), p. 102 (RMWC).

p. 176, "After freedom they began to die . . ." Avary, *Dixie After the War,* p. 195.

p. 177, "Ignorant negroes, or tools of corrupt men . . ." Sarah Rice Pryor, MS Collection, 24061, VSL.

p. 177, "But we had to work hard with darkies . . ." Jane B. Springs to M. E. Springs, November 4, 1888, Springstein, South Carolina, Childs Family Collection, SCL.

p. 178, "southern fanatics rode that hobby everywhere . . ." Catherine Clinton, "Reconstructing Freedwomen," Clinton and Silber, *Divided Houses,* p. 315.

p. 178, "No wonder then, that the cry is loud . . ." January 6, 1866, *Colored American* (Augusta, Georgia).

p. 179, "Many a man and woman in the

South have lived in wedlock . . ." W.E.B. DuBois, *Darkwater: Voices from Within the Veil* (New York: Harcourt, Brace, 1921), p. 172.

p. 180, "a squad of blacks marched, bound the owner . . ." Avary, *Dixie after the War,* p. 267.

p. 180, "we are informed that a most fiendish outrage . . ." January 27, 1866, *Loyal Georgian* (Augusta, Georgia), p. 2.

p. 180, "there is little call for female help . . ." June 30, 1866, BRF&AL, M1048, reel 10, 0580.

p. 180, Angaline Robbins, August 15, 1867, Greensboro, Georgia, BRF&AL, M798, reel 17.

p. 180, Cornelia Whitley, January 6, 1866, Gordonsville, Virginia, BRF&AL, M1048, reel 12, 0073.

p. 180, "it is my earnest conviction that they are . . ." Colonel W. M. Smith to E. B. Washburne, December 17, 1865, Magnolia, BRF&AL, M826, reel 17.

p. 181, "If it needs lynching to protect . . ." Rebecca Latimer Felton, see LeeAnn Whites, *Georgia Historical Quarterly* (summer 1992), p. 369.

p. 185, "this magnificent memorial . . ." Angie Parrot, "Love Makes Memory Eternal: The United Daughters of the Confederacy in Richmond, Va., 1897–1920." Edward Ayers and John C. Willis, *The Edge of the South: Life in Nineteenth-Century Virginia* (Charlottesville: University of Virginia Press, 1991), p. 220.

THE ROAD TO TARA

p. 191, "This is the story of life on a plantation located . . ." Olive Taylor Cardwell, *Life on a Plantation* (Lynchburg, Va.: Blanch Gibbs Dolls, 1968), p. 1 (RMWC).

p. 193, "Southern women are not simply pivotal . . ." See Kathryn Lee Seidel,

The Southern Belle in the American Novel (University Press of Florida, 1985).

p. 198, "I am no apologist for slavery . . ." Eliza Ripley, *Social Life, in Old New Orleans: Being Recollections of My Girlhood* (New York: D. Appleton, 1912), p. 210.

p. 198, "they fought all day just a block . . ." Darden Pyron, *Southern Daughter* (New York: Oxford University Press, 1991), p. 32.

p. 200, "In one of my rare visits South . . ." See unpublished essay by Michele Gillespie, Agnes Scott College.

p. 200, "Good morning, Aunt Susan . . ." N. G. Daingerfield, *Frescati: A Page From Virginia History* (New York: Neale Publishing Company, 1909), p. 12 (RMWC).

p. 200, "Yes, Dorothy dear, a lot of children . . ." Sallie Southall Cotten, *Negro Folk Lore Stories* (Charlotte, N.C.: Queen City Printing Company, 1923), p. 2 (RMWC).

p. 201, "KIDNAPPER! . . ." Henrietta Daingerfield, *Our Mammy,* p. 103 (RMWC).

p. 201, "Poor little children nowadays . . ." Cotten, *Negro Folk Lore Stories,* p. 4.

p. 201, "the blind woman's quick ear . . ." Daingerfield, *Frescati,* p. 18.

p. 203, "These vivid stereotypes . . ." See Kenneth Goings, *Mammy and Uncle Mose* (Bloomington: Indiana University Press, 1994).

p. 205, "Southerns." See Edward Campbell, Jr., *The Celluloid South: Hollywood and the Southern Myth* (Knoxville: University of Tennessee Press, 1981).

p. 211, "T-A-R-A." I would like to thank Eric Foner, the Dewitt Clinton Professor of Columbia University, for his observation.

Illustration Credits

⟡

Cover, LC #J7-NC-2175, LC #BH83201-2492; p. 2, MPAAS; pp. 4–5, LC #B811-211; pp. 12–13, VHS; p. 14, MoMA, p. 17, AHS; p. 18, SCHS; p. 19, author's collection; p. 20 top, MOC; p. 20 bottom, R. Alex Wells; Courtesy Missouri Department of Natural Resources; Archives of the Confederate Memorial State Historic Site; p. 21, author's collection; p. 22 top, RMWC; p. 22 bottom, author's collection; p. 23, Sven Arnstein, Courtesy RHI Entertainment; Inc.; pp. 24–25, NYHS; p. 26, SCHS; p. 28, *Harper's Weekly Illustrated* 7/13/61; p. 30, HNO; p. 32, LC #USZ62-31015; p. 33, Edward King, *Sketches of the South* (1875); p. 35, HNO; p. 36, Bourne, *Pictures of Slavery* (1834), LC #USZ62-30851; p. 37, NYHS; p. 38, Bourne, *Pictures of Slavery* (1834), LC #USZ62-30825; p. 39, LC #US762-48170; p. 40, MoMA; p. 42, HNO; p. 43, MOC; p. 45, LC #B8171-502; p. 46, Edward King, *Sketches of the South* (1875); p. 47, LC #USZ62-13954; p. 48, *Harper's Weekly Illustrated* 5/4/61; pp. 50–51, LC #B8184-7721; p. 52, USMHI; p. 54, author's collection; p. 55, USMHI; p. 57, MOC; p. 58, *Harper's Weekly Illustrated* 8/10/61; p. 60, *Harper's Weekly Illustrated* 6/7/62; p. 61, *Harper's Weekly Illustrated* 6/14/62; p. 53, *Harper's Weekly Illustrated* 3/9/61; p. 64, MOC; p. 67, MoMA; p. 68 top, NA #200S-CC-657; p. 68 bottom, LC #B8171-526; p. 70, LC; p. 71, LC #USZ62-2571; p. 72, HNO; p. 73, LC #B811-211; p. 74, LC #B811-2299; p. 75, LC #B811-2300; pp. 76–77, *Harper's Weekly Illustrated* 11/12/61; p. 78, Courtesy of South Carolina History and Relic Room, Columbia, South Carolina; p. 81, MOC; p. 82, MOC; p. 84, Edward King, *Sketches of the South* (1875); p. 86, MOC; p. 87, LC #B815-898; p. 89, MOC; p. 90, *Harper's Weekly Illustrated* 4/4/63; p. 92, *Harper's Weekly Illustrated* 10/12/61; p. 94, LC #BH83201-2492; p. 95, NA # CW 8664; p. 99, *Harper's Weekly Illustrated* 7/12/62; p. 102, LC #USZ-62-33005; p. 104, AHS; p. 105, HNO; pp. 106–07 USMHI; p. 108, NYHS; p. 111, LC #B8171-518; p. 114, LC #B811-2546; p. 117, LC #USZ62-33003; p. 119, USMHI; p. 120, LC #B8171-7745; p. 121, MOC; p. 124, *Harper's Weekly Illustrated* 11/16/61; p. 126, SCHS; p. 127, *Harper's Weekly Illustrated* 1/24/63; p. 128, LC #B8171-783; p. 129, LC #USZ62-32501; p. 133, NA #CW12; p. 134, MOC; pp. 136–37, LC #USZ62-37282; p. 138, MOC; p. 140, MOC; p. 141, Edward King, *Sketches of the South* (1875); p. 143, MOC; p. 144, MOC; p. 146 top, LC #B817-313; p. 146 bottom, LC #B8171-3428; p. 150, MOC; p. 151, *Harper's Weekly Illustrated* 12/24/64; p. 154, *Harper's Weekly Illustrated* 6/14/62; p. 157, *Harper's Weekly Illustrated* 10/26/61; p. 158, VMI; pp. 160–61, LC #B8184-10256; p. 162, SCHS; p. 164, MPAAS; p. 165, MPAAS; p. 166, Courtesy of Arthur Barrett, USMHI; p. 167 top, LC #J7SC-1431; p. 167 bottom, LC #USZ62-22076; p. 169, MoMA; p. 170, NYHS; p. 172, NYHS; p. 173, SCHS; p. 175, RMWC; p. 176, RMWC; p. 177, MOC; p. 178, LC #USZ62-8461; p. 179, LC #USZ62-35744; p. 181, LC #USZ62-30824; p. 182, VHS; p. 184, MOC; p. 185, MOC; p. 186, MOC; p. 188-89, MPAAS; p. 190, RMWC; p. 192, LC #J7-NC-2175; p. 193, author's collection; p. 195, RMWC; p. 196, RMWC; p. 197, LC; p. 198, RMWC; p. 199, VHS; p. 201, RMWC; p. 203, RMWC; p. 204, RMWC; pp. 205–07, MoMA; pp. 208–211, author's collection.

Index

Piggot, Emmeline, 90
"pilgrimage weeks," 187
Pinckney, Charles, Jr., 30
Pinckney, Charles, Sr., 29–30
Pinckney, Eliza Lucas, 29–30
Pinckney, Thomas, 30
Pinckney House, Charleston, S.C., *160–61*
Pinkerton agents, 93
Plantation Burial, 30
plantation mistresses, 29–31, 40–44, *42,* 79; afraid of their slaves, 118–19; burdens and responsibilities of, 38, 40–42, 43, 81; childbearing of, 43; Confederacy as viewed by, 62; Confederate soldiers hosted by, 122; decline in cotton prices and, 154; deprived of slaves, 121; dispirited by Confederate defeats, 132–33; forced into closer contact with black women, 134–35; and husbands' sexual liaisons with slaves, 38; nursing duties of, 82–89; rape feared by, 128, 130; as refugees, 130–32; remaining on land during war, 102, 109–10, 112–14, 115; Roman matron as cultural ideal of, 41; sacrifices of, 149–52; social isolation of, 44; transformation from belle to, 42–43; treasure buried or hidden by, 124; volunteerism of, 81–82; Yankees' contact with, 122–28, 130. *See also* Southern women
plantations: attempts to lure freedmen back to, 171–73; building of, 29; cash crops abandoned for foodstuffs by, 109; contributing to Confederate cause, 122; as depicted in popular culture, 21–23, 191–98, 202–4, 206–13; expanded westward, 38–40; legend of, 191–94; liberation of slaves from, 111, 119, 131; manpower shortages and, 115, 116; in postwar period, *162,* 171–73; preservation of values of, 187; rebellion of black labor force on, 110, 118–19;

scorched earth policy and, 110–12, 123–25; slaves absconding from, 31–32, 66–71, 73–74, 103, 116, 118, 119–21; slaves turned off land by, 102, 121; "twenty Negro law" and, 115, 140–41; during war, 109–35
planters: liaisons between slave women and, 35–38, 128–29; nonslaveholding whites' relations with, 44–46; paternalism ascribed to, 21; sacrifices of, 140–41; wealth and status of, 29
"Pocket Handkerchief War," 142
Poison Springs, Ark.: battle of (1864), 133
Pollard, E. A., 196
Poole, Ellie, 93
postcards, *193, 208*
pregnancies: medical dangers of, 43; of slave women, 34
Presley, Elvis, 28
Preston, Margaret Junkin, 112, 147
Price, Birch and Co., *74, 75*
Princess of the Moon, The (Ives), 195
prisoners of war, 83–84, 155–56
Pryor, Sarah Rice, 88, 154–55, 177

Q

Queen, 208

R

race relations: movie depictions of, 206, *207;* in Reconstruction, 166, 174–82; romanticized depictions of, *134,* 174–76, *176, 177,* 197–98, *198, 199,* 200, 201; in Union ranks, *50–51, 55,* 71; wartime dislocations and, 134–35
Radcliffe, Laura, 93
Raintree County, 40
Raleigh, Sir Walter, 28
Raleigh Register, 58, 92
rape, 128–30

Reconstruction, 165–81; ban on contact between Southern women and Union troops in, 166–68; emigration during, 168–69; interracial sex as issue in, 178–80, *181;* loyalty oath in, 170, *170;* marital problems during, 173–74; mental illness and suicide in, 174; Northern view of politics in, *178;* race relations in, 166, 174–82; rights granted to freed-people in, 165–66, 176–78; tales of poverty and harrowing woes in, 169–71; Union occupation in, 166–68, 177

refugees, *68, 130–32, 133,* 144, 145, 154–55, 159

Reid, Mary Lou, 54

Reminiscences (Taylor), 104

Revolutionary War, 30, 55, 56; slaves emancipated during, 31–32

rice, 29

Rice, Spottswood, 73–74

rice raft, *214–15*

Richmond, 65, 142, 144; bread riot in (1863), 153; Confederate White House in, *64;* "Massing of the Flag" ceremony in, 186

Richmond City Hospital, *87*

Richmond Enquirer, 140

Ridley, Rebecca, 122

Ripley, Eliza, 198

Rise and Fall of the Confederate Government, The (Davis), 21

Rives, William Cabell, 116

Roanoke Island, 27–28

Robbins, Angaline, 180

Robertson, John, 85

Robertson Hospital, Richmond, 85

Rogers, John, *170*

Rogers, Loula Kendall, 175

Rolle, Esther: as Mammy, *23*

Roosevelt, Theodore, 56

Roots, 208

Rose, Willie Lee, 116

Ruffin, Edmund, 174

Rutherford, Mildred Lewis, *184*

S

saboteurs, 89–90

sacrifices: camaraderie and fellowship associated with, 148–49; hair-donation scheme and, 143; minor deprivations portrayed as, 147; of planter aristocrats, 140–41; and Rebel balloon made of petticoats, 142–43; religious rhetoric and, 155; romanticism in depictions of, 149–50; scarcity of food and supplies and, 144, 149–54; of slave children, 148; Vicksburg campaign and, 156–58; of white children, 144–45; of white women, 139–55

salt, 152–53

Sanitary Commission, 80

Savannah Volunteer Guards, 103

Scales, Cordelia, 123

Scantling, Eliza, 148

Scarlett, 23, 208

scorched earth policy, 110–12, 123–25, 145–47

Scribner's Magazine, 33, 46, 196

Seabrook's Warehouse Hospital, Richmond, 88

Sea Islands: black community on, 116–17

Searching for Arms, 124

Secesh Industry, 60

Secessionists, *47,* 47–48, 53–54, 62

Selma Reporter, 59

Selznick, David O., 205, 209

Seven Days battles (1862), 142

Seven Pines, Va.: battle at (1862), 89

sexual relations: interracial, 35–38, 128–29, *129,* 178–80, *181,* 199, 207, *207;* rape and, 128–30

Shadowland, 194

Shelton Laurel massacre, 154

Sherman, Mrs. William T., 134

Sherman, William Tecumseh, 101–2, 110, 118, 134, 141

Sherman's March, *68,* 101–2, *102,* 110, 111, 155–56

Sherwood Plantation, Roanoke, Va.: reunion at, *12–13*

V

Van Lew, Elizabeth, 97
Varinaland, Va., *114*
Vaughn, Mary, 113–14
Velazquez, Loreta Janeta, 100
Venezuela, 169
Vicksburg, Miss.: battle of (1863), 111, 156–58
Victor, Mrs., 192–93
Victoria, queen of England, 93
Virginia: split apart over secession issue, 53
Virginia Company, 29
voting rights, 165, 176–77; for women, 181, 184

W

Walker Plantation, *106–7*
Wall, Mary, 133
Warner, Jack, 205
Warren, Robert Penn, 206–7
Washington, Denzel, 16
Washington, George, 30
Washington College, 83
Wells-Barnett, Ida B., 198–200

Wesleyan College, Macon, Ga., 166
West Point, 48
West Virginia: formation of, 53
Whalley-Kilmer, Joanne: as Scarlett, *23*
White, John, 27–28
white supremacy, 181–82
Whitley, Cornelia, 180
Wilkinson, Alfred, Jr., 168
William and Mary College, 183
Williamson, Mary, 61–62
Woman in Battle, The (Velazquez), 100
women: suffrage for, 181, 184. *See also* African-American women; plantation mistresses; slave women; Southern women
Women Dressed in Gay Colors, 141
Women of the South in War Times (Andrews), 175, 183
Woodward, C. Vann, 16
Woody, Mrs., 147
Works Progress Administration (1935–39), Work Projects Administration (1939–43) (WPA), 17, 164, 197–98
Worthington, Amanda, 113, 123, 147
Worthington, Bert, 113
Wright, Mary, 99–100

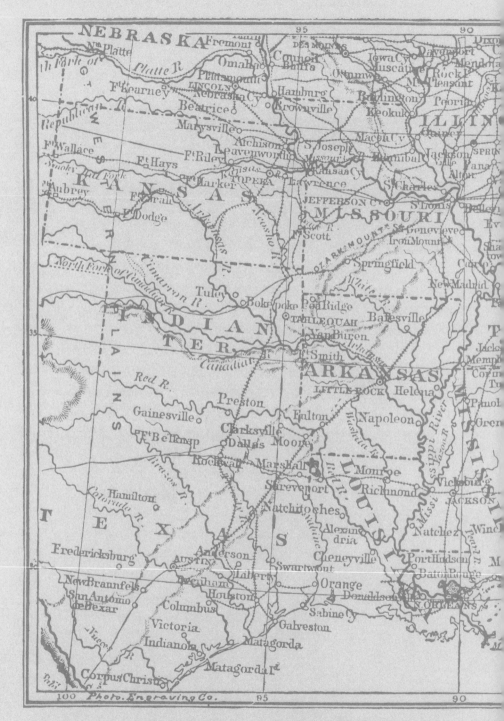

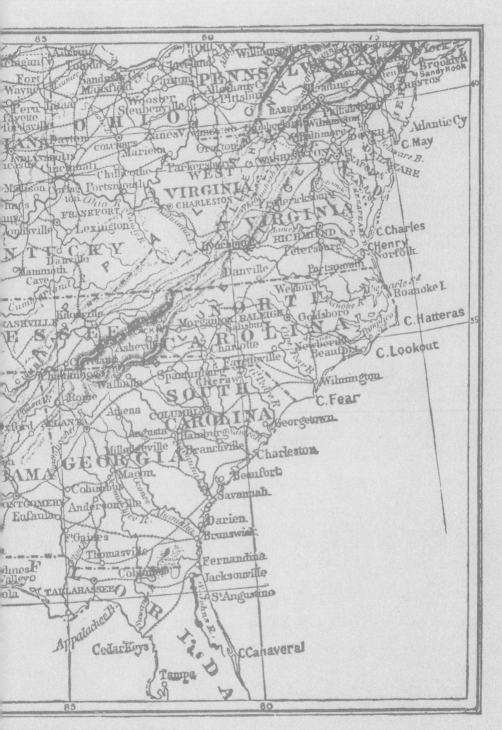

OUTHERN STATES.